'*The Season* is marked by her unsp........ detail and that superpower of detachment—a narrator who sees everything yet who is also deeply involved in the story, with emotional flourishes that rise when she watches her grandson.' *Age*

'Startling in its candour and compelling in its nakedness…a marvellous paean to the glories of youth just shy of the treacheries of manhood.' *Australian* on *The Season*

—

'Garner is one of those wonderful writers whose voice one hears and whose eyes one sees through. Her style, conversational but never slack, is natural, supple and exact, her way of seeing is acute and sympathetic, you receive an instant impression of being in the company of a congenial friend and it is impossible not to follow her as she brings to life the events and feelings she is exploring.' Diana Athill

'Not long ago I read Helen Garner for the first time and was so stunned that I wanted to run around the block; how strange, how wonderful, that a book can still make me feel that way.' Rumaan Alam

'There are very few writers that I admire more than Helen Garner.' David Nicholls

'Reading these snatches of life being lived is like being given a painting you love gleaming with the still-wet paint.' Helen Elliott

'Anything and everything she writes is a life lesson in courage, acuity and the eviscerating quest for self-knowledge.' Clare Wright

'The sensory nature of her observations is glorious.'
Guardian

'The sharpest of observers capturing with nuance and detail the most telling interactions between friends, siblings, lovers and society.'
Canberra Times

'Garner's [diaries] are spare, quiet, reflective: a portrait of the artist and her world, observed with scrupulous honesty.' Brenda Niall

'Garner is a natural storyteller.'
James Wood, *New Yorker*

'Her prose is wiry, stark, precise, but to find her equal for the tone of generous humanity one has to call up writers like Isaac Babel and Anton Chekhov.' *Wall Street Journal*

'Helen Garner [is] our greatest contemporary practitioner of observation, self-interrogation and compassion. Everything she writes, in her candid, graceful prose, rings true, enlightens, stays.'
Joan London

'Her use of language is sublime.' *Scotsman*

'There's no denying the force of her storytelling.'
Telegraph

'A voice of great honesty and energy.'
Anne Enright

'Garner's spare, clean style flowers into
magnificent poetry.' *Australian Book Review*

'She has a Jane Austen–like ability to whizz
an arrow straight into the truest depths of human
nature, including her own.' *Life Sentence*

'Compassionate and dispassionate in
equal measure…She writes with a profound
understanding of human vulnerability, and of the
subtle workings of love, memory and remorse.'
Economist

'She watches, imagines, second-guesses,
empathises, agonises. Her voice—intimate yet
sharp, wry yet urgent—inspires trust.' *Atlantic*

'The words almost dance off the page.'
Launceston Examiner

'Garner writes with a fearsome, uplifting grace.'
Metro UK

'A combination of wit and lyricism that is
immensely alluring.' *Observer*

'Honest, unsparing and brave.' *New York Times*

Helen Garner writes novels, stories, screenplays and works of non-fiction. In 2006 she received the inaugural Melbourne Prize for Literature, and in 2016 she won the prestigious Windham–Campbell Prize for non-fiction. She was honoured with the Australia Council Award for Lifetime Achievement in Literature in 2019. And in 2023 she was awarded the ASA Medal for her outstanding contribution to Australian literature. Her works include *Monkey Grip*, *The Children's Bach*, *The First Stone*, *Joe Cinque's Consolation*, *The Spare Room*, *This House of Grief* and three volumes of her diaries. She lives in Melbourne.

HELEN GARNER
The Season

TEXT PUBLISHING MELBOURNE AUSTRALIA

The Text Publishing Company acknowledges the Traditional Owners of the country on which we work, the Wurundjeri people of the Kulin Nation, and pays respect to their Elders past and present.

textpublishing.com.au

The Text Publishing Company
Wurundjeri Country, Level 6, Royal Bank Chambers, 287 Collins Street, Melbourne Victoria 3000 Australia

Published by The Text Publishing Company, 2024
Reprinted 2024

Book design by W. H. Chong
Cover photograph by Tim Bell
Typeset by J&M Typesetting

Printed and bound in Australia by Griffin Press, a member of the Opus Group. The Opus Group is ISO/NZS 14001:2004 Environmental Management System certified.

ISBN: 9781922790750 (paperback)
ISBN: 9781922791818 (ebook)

A catalogue record for this book is available from the National Library of Australia.

The paper this book is printed on is certified against the Forest Stewardship Council® Standards. Griffin Press, a member of the Opus Group, holds chain of custody certification SCS-COC-001185. FSC® promotes environmentally responsible, socially beneficial and economically viable management of the world's forests.

The Season

'I exalt the pagan personae of athlete and warrior…
whose ethic is candor, discipline, vigilance and valor.'
CAMILLE PAGLIA

'Don't turn your back on the play.'
TOM & NED'S DAD

I pull up at the kerb. I love this park they train in. I must have walked the figure-of-eight round its ovals hundreds of times, at dawn, in winter and summer, to throw the ball for Dozer, our red heeler—but he's buried now, in the backyard, under the crepe myrtle near the chook pen.

The boy jumps out with his footy and trots away, bouncing it. *Boy?* Look at him. He's been playing with our suburban club since he was a tubby little eight-year-old; I have never paid more than token attention to his sporting life. But this year he's in the Under-16s. The shoulders on him! He must be almost six feet tall. He's the youngest of my three grand-children. The last, and there will be no more.

—

At breakfast time I say, 'Can I start coming to training?'

'What? Why?'

'I don't know. I've got no work. I'm burnt out. I don't know what to do with myself. I need something to write about.'

'You better ask the coach.'

'Who's the coach?'

'We've got a new one. It's Archie.'

'What? The Archie we know? Isn't he only a boy? How old is he?'

'About twenty,' says Amby's mum, who remembers important facts.

Can you be a coach when you're only five years older than the players?

—

Under an umbrella outside the cafe, tall and skinny, white T-shirt and baseball cap: is that him? I come up behind him and he turns. Pale skin, bright blue eyes with black lashes. Face-splitting grin. Clever, funny, jumping out of his skin; ready to pick up a thought and go with it. 'Footy,' he says, 'is the most hilariously unnatural sport. Running *backwards*!' He's at uni. He gets what I'm after.

'Will I have to ask the club?'

'Nah. Just turn up.'

'What about the players?'

'Helen. They're fifteen. They're boys. They won't care. And five minutes later they'll have forgotten you were even there. They're fifteen-year-old boys trying to be men.'

He tips back his head in a fit of laughter.

—

All my life I've fought men, lived under their regimes, been limited and frustrated by their power; but in the first decade of the century I became a grandmother to a girl and two boys, a hands-on nanna who by some unimaginable miracle was invited to buy the house next door, knock down the fence, and become part of family life.

The girl and I understood each other at first glance. But having never raised a son, I now began to learn about boys and men from a fresh angle, to see their delicacy, their fragility, what they're obliged to do to themselves in order to live in this world, the codes of behaviour they've had to develop in order to discipline and sublimate their drive to violence.

The pandemic came. Melbourne copped more lockdowns than any other city in the nation. That's when footy really got a grip on me. It made me feel lucky to be alive. I learnt that when the chips are down, football rises. I saw that it's a kind of poetry, an ancient common language between strangers, a set of shared hopes and rules and images, of arcane rites played out at regular intervals before the citizenry. It revives us. It sustains us. In a time of fear and ignorance, it holds us above the abyss. And I started to glimpse what is grand and noble, and admirable and graceful about men.

But I keep quiet about this, because I don't want people to think I'm romanticising it, or to reproach me for not writing about women's footy. And I have to admit that, more than anything, this is about me and my grandson. Now that I've reached the age at which my mother died demented, now that my hearing and my eyesight are packing up and I can feel my memory starting to lose its grip, I need a reason to be near him, in the last years of his childhood. I want to know him better before it's too late, to learn what's in his head, what drives him; to see what he's like when he's out in the world, when he's away from his family, which I am part of; so in order to learn about his other life, I'm going to have to find a way to efface myself, to become a silent witness.

February

At five o'clock on a late summer afternoon I drive him to the first pre-season training of the year. His thighs are so long that his knees almost press against the glove box.

'Do you get nervous before training?'

'No.'

'Before a match?'

'Yes. I get nervous for days before a match and on the morning of the game when I wake up. But as soon as you get out there on the ground, it's all gorn.'

In no other context does he pronounce *gone* like this. Is it a football thing?

'What position do you play?'

'Midfield, mostly.'

'I don't even know what that means.'

'It means I'm always on the ball. I get plenty of action. Unless I'm tagging someone.'

What is tagging? I don't want to admit to him that although

I have followed the Western Bulldogs with a passion since before he was born I still hardly understand the rules.

The air is parched. Everything is standing still, bearing down. Boys are gathering slowly on the oval. I let him get out first. No boy would want to arrive at training with his nanna in tow. Away he jogs, shouldering his bag.

Where am I going to put myself, with my brand-new notebook hidden in the back pocket of my overalls? There are no seats. Wait, there's one, near the goalposts and the water bubbler at the western end, a big old-fashioned park bench made of thick wooden slats. When I sit on it, the metal boundary rail cuts straight across my line of vision. I hoist myself up on to the high, curved back of the bench and perch there, looking around.

This is the inner west. The air is full of a low metallic noise. Twenty metres behind me skateboarders are gliding up and down their steep curves of concrete. Suburban trains clatter back and forth along the southern edge of the park. On the other side of the raised railway track lies a vast tunnel excavation and construction site. Earth-moving behemoths roll ponderously, men march about in hi-vis and helmets. Beyond the site rise the blocky tops of many-coloured containers, the odd crane. An ambulance siren wails past, coming up from the river. What the hell am I doing here?

Archie the coach strides past my possie and flashes me a smile. I'm surprised to hear myself say, 'Hey, boss.' He begins to lay out near the goals a series of white plastic cones. A man with two dogs on leads ducks under the boundary fence and barges right through his careful pattern.

As the boys gather round the coach I start to notice physical types: one with a distance-runner's sinewy legs and a cloud of curly fair hair like the Western Bulldogs' Cody Weightman, an icon in our house; another blond one, shy-looking, skinny and fine, a head shorter than the rest but wiry; an Asian boy, composed and watchful, with a strikingly adult face and a smooth black ponytail.

They are busy now handling the new-looking yellow footballs. I will never understand the physics of it: how they can run and bounce them like that and get the wonky oval ball to obey them so they never pause or trip or stumble.

A late arrival in a Bloods T-shirt drops on to his back in the grass and takes a selfie; the low sun catches a big 'diamond' in his earlobe. His teammates, ignoring him, form two circles and start a manic handball drill, shouting each other's names in triplets, in nasal, broken voices: 'TommyTommyTommy. NedNedNed. XavierXavierXavier.'

The dull roar from the construction site cuts out. A tiny warm breeze passes from the north. A magpie warbles. An Indian woman in sports clothes walks past me murmuring an unbroken monologue into her phone. I could sink into a summer-evening trance. But the coach shouts, 'Boys. It's full contact and we'll go hard.' I sit up.

A boy does a bad kick, a real dud. 'Hopeless,' he mutters, and leans forward in a posture of shame.

The coach says, 'That's a dollar.'

Fast play, now. The smell of the grass they're crushing

reaches me. I'm fully awake. A boy takes a clean mark and I hear myself hiss: 'Yessss!' Someone spits. The first mozzie of the evening stings my arm. The coach leaps into the game, twists like a dancer, handballs behind him. His greater height, his greater skill. His cap flips half off his head; he snatches it and flings it back over his shoulder with his left hand while casually marking the ball in his right. A running boy sees the cap on the grass, pauses, looks down at it respectfully: the coach's cap. Should he pick it up? No. He straightens and runs on. Between bouts of action whoever is holding the ball will spin and flip it from hand to hand: it's always moving.

Balls in a final kick to kick are flying all over the place. Amby is way over there on my right, close to the southern boundary. I see him take a mark and turn to two hi-vis tradies who are leaning over the fence, calling out to him. He veers away from them laughing and sinks his boot into the ball.

It's hot. They train for only an hour. Driving away from the park I chuck an illegal U-ey and halfway into my turn see a car heading east at speed. I have to swerve into the parking lane to avoid a collision.

'Shit,' I say. 'That was a dumb piece of driving.'

'It was Archie.'

'Oh no. Did he see it was me?'

'Yes. He looked right at me and laughed.'

From the kerb I text him a shame emoji: 'I don't usually drive like that.'

'Ha ha,' he replies. 'Don't worry I didn't see anything.'

—

Back at our place I'm knocking up tuna rice for tea when Amby's older brother walks in from university O-week, looking cool and interesting in his black singlet. He says he's met some people and they'd been planning to go to a club, but he would have had to wait around for four hours, so he decided to come home. 'I'm fatigued,' he says. 'Not just tired. Fatigued.' He and Amby compare notes on this distinction.

Next morning at breakfast Amby complains grandly of his soreness.

'Were you aware of me watching?'

'Yes.'

'What, all the time?'

'Yes.'

'Oh damn. I was hoping that wouldn't happen.'

'I wasn't distracted. It inspired me to do cool things so I'd be in the book.'

—

As wallpaper on my phone I've got a press photo of the Western Bulldogs' captain, Marcus Bontempelli, at a moment of defeat, helping Josh Bruce off the ground after his already replaced knee has given way. Bont's arm is around his teammate, his cheek pressed against the stumbling man's shoulder: their huge spread hands, Bruce's ragged man-bun falling in strands, his face lowered in pain and despair. I was once reproached

by all my grandchildren for having in my phone a photo of
three U10 players leaving the field at the final siren: two of
them towered over the one in the middle, a very small boy
whose bravery I greatly admired. They shouted at me: it was
'disturbing', they said, that I had this photo of a child in my
phone. *What?* I was furious, I argued with all my force, but
they got me on the ropes, and their parents supported them:
'How would *you* feel, Hel, if some stranger had a photo of
you in their phone?' In my heart I never bowed to them, but
I pretended to, to keep the peace. And now I show Amby
the photo of Bont and Bruce, this Homeric scene of broth-
erly tenderness and care, and I say in a mocking tone, 'Is it
"disturbing" to you, that I've got this photo in my phone?'

He looks at it, recognises it. 'No,' he says, declining to bite.
'I love that photo.'

—

'Is Collingwood the only AFL team with a curse on it?' says
my friend, an aesthetically sophisticated woman of my age
who doesn't care a fig for footy but knows the ancient myths
and sees the point of them. 'The curse of being working class?
The brutal frontline fighters. The Bulldogs are the boys from
Sparta, small, leaner, better-contained—they're the second
line. But the boys from Melbourne...maybe they're cursed by
their heritage of pomp?'

I can take any amount of this.

'Football's a mirror of war,' she says, 'a mirror we can look into safely. And the reason people are so crazy about this particular mirror is that war is as close as we ever get to being in the midst of life and death simultaneously. It's some sort of critical human state being played out. At an unconscious level. *I am alive now—I could die in an hour.'*

I send her a photo of the Western Bulldogs' Ed Richards, and ask her the right word for the colour of his magnificent red hair.

'I'd call it titian,' she replies. 'Once I stopped a thirteen-year-old boy on the street in Gisborne, who had this hair colour. He called it "chestnut, and not mahogany".'

Ed Richards, she thinks, looks 'sweet, modest, noble. Which phalanx would he be best in?'

I go to the Bulldogs' website and watch Ed Richards highlights edited into a flow. His dark-burning hair against the bright green of the grass. His speed and grace. How the hell do they keep *running* for all that time?

—

Second pre-season training, a Monday. The boys seem further away today, smaller. Wind out of the south-west, different from last time, steady and cool. I've got a coat and I'm grateful for it. I can't sense what's going on. A lot of handball. Trains are drowning out the coach's voice, the wind squeals in my hearing aids. Angus, the tall thin boy in the Bloods T-shirt, has had a buzz cut since last time. Where's his flashy earring? Stripped of the softness of hair he looks younger, paler. Magpies peck at the turf. Mynahs squabble on the boundary fence. My teeth would be chattering with cold if I wasn't clenching them. I'm dismayed: is this boring? Am I bored? I am very rarely bored. I'm not the boreable *type*. Then it strikes me that this is the essence of the thing I'm studying: constant changes of mood and condition.

Amby is disconsolate on the drive home. Staggering into the kitchen, sweaty and mad at himself for not having done well on the field, he looks around wildly and says, 'I know what I want. I want SOUP!' And of course there is none. But next time there will be.

—

One afternoon, after school, I come across Amby lying on his back, out on the deck.

'Are you thinking of love songs?'

'No. I just watched a sad movie. Well, it wasn't sad, but it made me think of sad things.'

'Like what?'

'I was thinking about how people want to be remembered.'

Only an hour before, I was lying on my bed reading Madeline Miller's *The Song of Achilles*, in tears because the sea nymph Thetis, Achilles' cold, angry mother, was refusing to allow the name of Patroclus, his shamed and exiled lover, to be written on Achilles' tombstone. I tell Amby the story, and by the end I'm having to cover my face and run inside, though Amby is not the sort of boy who thinks it's stupid to cry over a story: only a few years ago he sobbed over *Red Dog*, when the dead man's kelpie trots tirelessly along the desert roads, searching, searching for his master. Thetis relents. 'Two shadows reaching through the hopeless heavy dusk…Their hands meet, and light spills in a flood, like a hundred golden urns pouring out the sun.' I think Amby would get it.

March

Training, Thursday 2 March. Now I'm starting to recognise, with pleasure, the citizens of the suburb whose custom it is to come to the park at this time of the evening: the buzz-cut middle-aged runner in his grey shorts and singlet; the old Indian couple wheeling their granddaughter in a pusher; the skateboarders with tatts and piercings and lurid clothing. Fresh wind coming from the south-west, from behind the raised railway line and the big containers piled beyond it.

A woman is standing near the goalposts, holding a clipboard. She has a warm, sweetly handsome face, long brown hair drawn back.

'How do you think they look?' she says.

'They're big! And their voices have all broken! I'm Amby's grandmother. Which one's yours?'

'Harvey. He's not here—he's still at cricket. There's a new one here today.'

'The one with reddish hair?'

'Yes, and purple shorts. I'd better get his details.'

She strolls on to the field with her dog on a lead, calls to the boy. He turns aside from the handball drill. His face softens as he gives her his name: Luis. He looks older than the others, his expression more mature.

The team's former coach, father of the blond brothers Tommy and Ned, is playing kick to kick behind the goals with a much smaller boy. He probably doesn't realise that he said one of the first things about footy that pulled me up short, that hooked me. One day last year he was leaning on the rail near me at some random game that I was pretending not to be bored by. I overheard him say under his breath: *'Don't turn your back on the play.'* After the siren I asked him what this meant. He said: 'A kid's taken a mark, right? And he's lining up a shot for goal. But because he's only concentrating on himself and his own chance to goal, he fails to notice that two of his teammates have moved around behind him into better positions to score. He kicks, and misses. By turning his back, he's let his teammates down.'

This evening his bare-legged four-year-old daughter, in a grubby black and white striped cotton dress, rushes to a goalpost and goes swarming up its padded section like a monkey, hauling herself, gripping the spongy white sheath with her knees and toes. She perches there, eight feet from the ground, gazing about in triumph, her fair curls standing up in a crest. A man in a black business suit and tie, very straight-backed and correct, goes sailing past beneath her on a scooter, oblivious.

The boys on the field are bursting with a crazy energy. When they run, at startling speed, their hair streams back off their brows and temples. They yell each other's names as they run and kick, they execute criss-cross figures of eight and handball drills so intricate my eye can hardly follow them. Every few minutes the coach shouts 'Drop!' and they fall to the ground, elbows flexed, and do half a dozen push-ups, out of sync with each other: for a moment the turf ripples with low, uneven waves of colour. They spring up, stand close and silent round the coach while he speaks, then explode apart in laughter. They jostle and shove and swear and bellow in their broken voices, roaring and hugging and pushing.

Something sharp turns in me. It's envy.

The cool air, the grey cloud cover with slits of pale blue. A train rattles past.

The former coach comes to lean beside me at the rail: 'What do you think?'

'They're so *tall*.'

'Yes. They look…good. And I think there's much less'—he stacks his two flat hands in the air in front of his face, six inches apart, then moves them towards each other, like something closing—'*difference* between them. Their skill levels.'

———

Monday training. They start at 6.10. Warm day, warm evening, so agreeable everyone is half-stunned, it's so gentle and sweet, so mild. Amby trains in ordinary street clothes—a big T-shirt, school shorts. On the field they're spread so far apart, it's like a dream; everything's slowed down. The yellow footballs glow soft and gold in the gentle autumn light.

Handball-out-of-a-tackle drill. Sometimes how like a dance! Their torsos turn and lift. The coach skips backwards on his graceful legs. At a quick break they rush to their bottles and guzzle. Water spills off their chins. Now handball in a ring. This is when they shout. The former coach, Tom and Ned's dad, always with one eye on his gravity-defying daughter, leans next to me at the rail.

'How do they learn to do that counter-intuitive thing,' I ask, 'to control the urge to throw?'

'The earlier you're taught, the better,' he says. 'If you don't start to play till you're thirteen, it takes much longer for it to become natural. I'm not that keen on it, to be honest. I think kicking's much more important. If you've got a team that's good at kicking and a team that's good at handballing, the kickers are going to win.'

A young woman in full make-up and firm-fitting black shorts and top goes jogging by: she's so smooth and perfect she ought to be in a nightclub. Twenty women jog past me, in lycra shorts and T-shirts with the slogan RUN LIKE A GIRL. I can hear their voices from a long way off, the music of them, some murmuring, others laughing and loud. A bunch of running women will talk; men tend to run in silence.

Long cool shadows are lying across the grass. The familiar locals have come out to take the evening air. They stroll along the path that encircles the ground. A girl of nine or so, with a fluffy white dog on a lead, grants me a formal nod. This evening, my fourth one, almost everyone who passes smiles at me. Perhaps one day soon I too will belong here.

The U18s are training at the other end of the ground. They pull on orange vests and 'verse' the U16s for half an hour. They are different, louder and heavier, no longer slender: they have thicker bodies and their legs are more solid. Suddenly I see our boys in a larger context. Their fineness seems valuable, precious, so soon to be swallowed up in manliness.

The boys are in pairs now, doing scissors paper rock. Archie shouts, 'Loser gets a bib, boys. Loser gets a bib.' They divide into two teams, and play. Goals are marked by plastic domes placed on the grass. This is what I love to watch, the manic repetitive drills opening out into surging, slanting runs, the running and bouncing, the running in arcs, the twisting break-out from a pack, the reaching for the mark, the seizing of the golden ball out of the air and the booting of it between the cones, the shouts, the jeers, the laughing.

When it's over they pick up their gear and peel away. One boy steps off the grass and straight on to the back of a scooter on which his brother has been waiting. Without a word they glide away, relaxed and loose.

In the car, Amby says, 'This is the best part, getting driven home. It used to be the worst part—oh, I hated it, having to slog up this hill.'

'Would you say that each training session has a different sort of mood?'

'Oh, absolutely. The worst ones are when nobody really

wants to be there—in winter, when it's cold and everybody's grouchy. But on a day like this, when it's warm, everyone's relaxed and in a good mood, you can mess around and make jokes, and it's fun.'

'What's all the shouting for?'

'Some kids don't like to shout, I don't know why. But we have to. You have to have a voice. So whoever's got the ball knows you're there.'

Now the penny drops about something my granddaughter said, years ago, when she played for Melbourne Uni and I was marvelling at the way players handball blindly, at top speed, in the press of a game: 'How do they know someone's there?'

'Oh, a lot of shouting goes on out there, Hel,' she said.

—

Amby comes into my kitchen. He and his dad are going out to buy him new boots.

'What have you been wearing to training?'

'Just ordinary runners.'

'What? Doesn't it hurt, all the kicking?'

He shrugs: 'No.'

'What's the difference between runners and proper boots?'

'Boots have got studs. They make it easier to, you know'— he demonstrates a dramatic sideways skid. 'You can turn faster; and stop; and you can—*accelerate*.'

Again, a stab of envy.

'Have you got a brush? A stiff one? I have to clean up my old boots. See if they still fit me.'

He produces them: dark blue, with stripes, and the famous studs. They're scarred and patterned all over with last season's mud. He must have pulled them off and slung them into the laundry last September, and there they lay for six months, filthy and forgotten, while his feet grew longer and wider, bit by bit, each day.

—

The young Englishwoman who cuts my hair, over in North-cote, tells me she plays AFL for a team in Richmond. I look at her with new respect.

'Did you study the rules first?'

'*Pfff*—no!'

'What, you just picked it up as you went along?'

'Pretty much. There's not all that many rules, in AFL. Compared to some other sports. Like netball, where you have to stay in a particular area.'

'Do they move you to different positions?'

'Yes, I'm usually on the wing, or at centre half-back. I didn't want to be in the ruck. I like running and I love tackling. I didn't want to play forward. Too much depends on you. And I don't want to play defence.'

'What was the hardest thing about learning to play?'

'It took me a long time to get that you're not allowed to fight your way out of a tackle.'

'Oh! You're not?'

'No—not like in other sorts of football. If someone tackled me I used to fight them'—she makes a sharp stabbing movement with one elbow—'like in rugby.'

Snipping away, she tells me about a girl who turns up to every one of their matches an hour and a half before the start and works her way, alone and silently, right across the ground, 'picking up liquor'.

My hearing aids are out of my ears, because of her scissors. 'What? *What* does she pick up?'

'Little stones, pebbles, bits of rubbish—litter. She never plays, but she's attached herself to the team, somehow. And she cleans the ground for us.'

'Wow. As if it was a shrine. That she purifies.'

She nods. Later, I will be surprised to find that not a single footy nut, male or female, to whom I describe this strange habit, even when I use the words *shrine* and *purify*, seems taken aback, let alone utters a scornful laugh.

—

Lunchtime at a table outside the cafe. 'What's the deal with tackling?'

'Right. Here are the rules. The first one is, not above the shoulders. That's called a high tackle and the tackled person gets a free. Second: you can't tackle below the knees. That's called a trip. It's not a real tackle. And the other guy gets a free.'

'Are there different sort of *styles* of tackling?'

'No. It's jumping and grabbing them and hoping they'll fall over. If you get the ball, I mean when it's not a mark but you get it, or you pick it up off the ground, and if you get tackled before you have a chance to get rid of it, that's a ball-up, not a free against you. It's called "no prior opportunity". That's those drills you like watching—they're about agility—how fast you can get the ball and give it off again.

'There are ways you can get a free from tackling. If the tackled person drops the ball. Or if the tackled person's "holding the ball"—fending off the tackler or sidestepping round him. There's no actual time limit—but if you try that while you're being tackled, that's called holding the ball.

'Another sort of free you can get against you is if you run too far without bouncing the ball. This is vague. As long as you keep bouncing, you can run the whole length of the ground. But it's hard to bounce and keep your speed up. For some reason people always slow down a bit when they're bouncing. Just say you're getting chased by someone, and people are yelling "You're hot!"—then you don't want to bounce, because if you bounce you'll slow down and you'll get tackled. If you slow down, the one chasing you will catch up and smash you into the ground. If you run too far without bouncing, because you don't want to slow down and get tackled, the umpire can blow the whistle and the other side gets a free.'

'Right. Okay. I get it. I *think* I get it.'

'Know what I've noticed? When I try to tackle someone and I don't do a good tackle, I can remember afterwards exactly what I've done—what I did wrong, how I could feel my arms slip off the guy and he runs away. But when I do a good tackle I can't really remember it. I think I must close my eyes when I tackle. I just grip, and even if I feel my hand sliding off, I grab my wrist with my other hand and I drag him to the ground. And then it's like I wake up. Like I was unconscious.'

'Is it a triumphant moment?'

'It is.'

'This reminds me of a famous sax player I read about once. He said, "When I play badly, it's my fault. But when I play well, it's got nothing to do with me."'

We sit quietly in the weak autumn sun. I wrap the crusts of my toastie in a paper napkin, to take home for the chooks. I'm about to put my notebook back in my bag when he starts again.

'I remember one very vivid one. We were playing against Sunshine. This little kid got the ball. I tackled him but he handballed it to one of his teammates. I got up and started chasing the other kid. I can remember coming in from the side, I remember he had a mullet down to like between his shoulder blades, he was quite short but very stocky and fast. And while I was coming towards him I knew he didn't know I was there. I tackled him, and I got a free kick because he dropped the ball. I remember that as one of the best feelings I've had in footy—I tackled the first guy and he got away, but I chased the second one and it paid off.'

—

At home we read in the *Age* about Liam Picken, the Western
Bulldogs player of endearing character and shining skills
who had to retire a few years ago at thirty-three: he had been
concussed too many times. He is now launching civil action
against the AFL, the Western Bulldogs and the club doctors.
His lawyers say that he was repeatedly returned to the field
after suffering concussion. They say he was never made aware
of test results that should have had him referred to concussion
experts or sent for brain scans. He didn't understand, they say,
the full extent of his injuries or his symptoms. He 'voiced his
concerns', but the medical advice he was given was that he was
still fit to play. It grieves us, and frightens us, to read about his
brain injury: he suffers from ongoing headaches, lethargy, irri-
tability, poor concentration, severe levels of depression, anxiety
and stress, and photophobia, an aversion to bright light.

Another Bulldogs player, Caleb Daniel, always wears a
leather helmet. A TV commentator in a tight blue suit flips
him a smart-arse question: 'What's with the helmet? Keeping
Mum happy?' Daniel doesn't bother to answer.

—

At a lunch party down in St Kilda a bunch of friends in their
seventies get talking about the recent upsurge of anxiety about
concussion in footy. A retired lawyer, all six-foot-four of him,
the sweetest, funniest guy you could hope to meet, quietly tells

a story from his long-ago years playing for Richmond. He gets knocked out cold on the field. He's on the ground. After an unknown amount of time he comes to, gets to his feet, and says to a passing teammate, 'Is this the Grand Final?'

'Yep.'

'Which way are we kicking?'

'That way.'

And he plays on to the end.

Is there a moral to this story? Nobody looks for one. We just laugh with him, almost tenderly.

—

At the arrival gate where I'm waiting for Amby and his mother, who are coming home from a couple of days in Adelaide, a man near me is holding a folded copy of the *Herald-Sun*. On its front page is a glorious close-up portrait of Bulldogs star Bailey Smith, king of the blond mullet, crouched on the turf in his sky-blue Dogs jumper and wrinkled white boots, one forearm across his thigh, the other hand spread and resting lightly on a Sherrin: despite his absurd little moustache (they're all growing them—it's a thing in the AFL and even on the streets, for God's sake) he looks older, stronger, darker, his gaze full of power, a calm awareness of his own beauty. 'EXCLUSIVE: Bulldogs star reveals how hitting rock bottom helped turn his life around'.

Amby, with his hood up, comes shambling off the plane behind his mum, towing a little suitcase.

'How was Womad?'

'It was great. There were lots of girls there, around my age. It was so cool, looking at them. I could think about having an affair with all of them when we had eye contact.'

'Wait till he takes his hood off,' says his mum.

Hang on—first he has the story. 'In the crowd,' he says, 'I could see someone holding up a broom handle. And on it was a sign that said FREE HAIRCUTS. And I thought, I'll get a mullet. For footy. So I go up to them. They're like, "Cool! We got someone!" The girl starts cutting. She's like, "These scissors are just from Kmart but they're really good."'

He drops the hood and turns his head: there it is, the mullet, his thick fair hair chopped rough as guts, his ears bared and his neck hidden, the top and front still floppy. A peasant boy in Tolstoy.

'Is it all right? Do you like it?'

'I love it. It's cool. What did she do with the hair?'

'She let it fall on the grass. And it blew away.'

—

'Hey, mullet-head,' I text. 'I can't come to training tonight.'

'No worries.'

'Mullet being approved at school?'

'Not really. Everyone thinks it's bad.'

'Pfff. Can you tough it out?'

'Yep.'

'Good on ya. Anyway they're all wrong. Maybe it needs a

bit of thinning out here and there but in general you're still super hot—ha ha burn this.'

'Thanks Helen.'

'Is that a crying emoji? Or a laughing till you cry one?'

(Half an hour later) 'Laughing till I cry.'

—

You can feel the season approaching. Everyone is wild-eyed and revved-up.

Every morning I turn straight to the footy pages. The way they talk! 'His dash and goal nous.' 'I will go down the park and have a kick; if someone is there for a kick I will have a kick.' 'He has never been an endurance athlete and the Bulldogs found he had maintained his power and burst.' 'I am not going to play safe, I will back myself in to have a crack.' 'A tough-nut half-back from Tasmania.' 'Soft-tissue setbacks.' 'Impressed on a wing.' 'I was very fortunate to captain a game when I was twenty ironically.' 'Looked a little ginger.' 'Unstoppable in the air.'

—

Can Toby Greene reshape his entire character if they make him captain of Greater Western Sydney? Personally, I will always hate his guts for gouging Bont's eyes and kicking Luke Dahlhaus in the jaw, but what a player he is; and a man at a party tells me I should take note of his efforts to get a grip, and reminds me of the effect on a bloke of the sort of father Greene's got.

—

I show my friend a three-quarter standing portrait of the Sydney Swans' Buddy Franklin: head turned to the camera, tattooed, stubbled, short-haired, straight-backed, severe, a tiny frown, holding a ball against his flank with his right hand, the left one hanging alert and relaxed in the air.

'It made me gasp,' she replies. 'I'm not sure what the emotion was, but I think a rather strong admiration for his masculinity.'

'I'm worried about Buddy. Please God he doesn't break down but can retire on his feet.'

This friend always says she doesn't care about footy—that is, about actual games. But I remind her of an afternoon years ago, when we were driving home from a walk along the river. We passed a suburban park on a hilltop over in Aberfeldie, and noticed a bunch of young boys, maybe U12s, training with their coach on the thick green grass. We pulled up and got out. No one else was around. There was a bench for us, under a leafy tree. We sat down to watch. I kept expecting one of us to get restless, to say, 'Okay, come on, let's go.' But neither of us did. Instead, we became calm. We must have stayed there for an hour, not saying anything much, just giving our attention. And when it started to get dark and we headed home, we both remarked on how peaceful it had been, and how much we'd loved sitting there.

'I remember that,' she says.

'It was a bit like being at a shrine, wasn't it.'

'*Shrine*?' She won't come at it. 'Not for me, it wasn't.'

Stubborn old atheist leftie.

—

Friday night at home. After stitching up a woollen rug we've knitted, a friend and I, tired and bug-eyed from hours of close work with the needles under a lamp, turn on the Collingwood/Geelong game for a quick look before we go to bed. She's Bombers, I'm Western Bulldogs: we have no skin in the game, we don't know the players' names or care who wins. We make idle observations about their haircuts and demeanour.

Then two men collide in the air and crash separately to earth. They lie there, motionless, two huge fallen statues. One drags himself to his feet, apparently unhurt, but the other, on his back, is writhing. Support people are running to him, a plump girl in shorts carrying a stretcher goes chugging across the grass. The other players draw back, move away. The cameras too are withdrawing. They don't know where to direct their gaze, they roam pointlessly here and there.

'Looks like he's broken his arm,' murmurs the commentator. 'We wouldn't want to go in close on something like this.'

Collingwood players stand on the boundary, waiting for news. One with long blond hair reaches forward to his teammate, whose headband has got twisted out of place, and gently corrects it. A chunky little tractor-like vehicle whizzes out to where the wounded man lies. The trainers load him on to it. As his teammates flood in around him, then disperse to get out of the way, I catch a tiny glimpse of his racked face, the panting rhythm of his shoulder.

—

Everyone else has gone to a big family party in Ocean Grove. Only me and Amby here to watch the Bulldogs versing Melbourne. I serve a soup made from the glut of zucchini in the backyard. He loafs on the couch and I take my usual position on the floor between the coffee table and the TV. I despise the crowd for booing Lachie Hunter because he has moved from the Bulldogs to the Demons. He looks all wrong in the darker blue Melbourne jumper. He has a fresh buzz cut and appears young and inexperienced. Which he is not. Someone kicks a goal and heads back to the centre, pointing and gesturing at invisible people and mouthing what look to me like commands: *Get over there—why aren't you over there?*

'What are they saying when they point and shout like that after a goal?'

Amby shrugs. 'Just random encouraging words, I guess.'

'I reckon this will be a worrying game, Amb.'

'Yep. It'll be a worrying game. So much of footy is worrying, actually.'

Aaron Naughton snatches a ball out of the air. 'What a grab!' shouts Amby. 'Holy shit!'

One player is wearing two black armbands. I suggest that two of his grandparents may have died. We regard him thoughtfully, eating our black sesame mochi.

'When I die, will you wear an armband?'

'*Yes.*'

The Demons' young forward Kysaiah Pickett gets a very dodgy free out of a clash with Tom Liberatore, kicks a goal from it, then turns and jeers right into Libba's face. Insolent pup. Very bad form for a young player no matter how gifted—and Pickett is a sublime player—to give cheek to a brilliant veteran like Liberatore. A tough, wily, reliable veteran. A *modest* veteran, with the self-command that stops him from decking the impudent youth on the spot.

Late in the game, which the Bulldogs are clearly losing, Pickett flares again: Bailey Smith takes a mark and kicks, and Pickett comes flying back at him through the air, spearing on an angle like a man flung out of a pub, hurling his entire body at Smith's torso, and mows him down. Bulldogs vice-captain, Jack Macrae, goes at Pickett with both arms out, mouthguard blazing white over his clenched teeth, and it's on. Teammates are tearing at the fighting men to part them, they're on the ground, the crowd's bellowing. Faintly we can hear the umpire's voice: 'He's on report. *He's on report.*'

—

Pickett gets a two-week suspension for his huge body blow on Smith. At home the others agree that this is right and fair.

They call that a *bump*? I don't think so. I say he should get a third week for jeering right in Libba's face.

'Pickett's a fabulous player,' I opine in headmistressly tones under the fig tree, 'but he ought to be taught some manners.'

Amby shakes his head sombrely.

Ah well, I've got a nanna's view of these matters.

I look to the *Age* sportswriter Greg Baum for sardonic good sense: '"I don't care what anyone says, the big bump is just a part of footy that I bloody love," tweeted former Carlton and Brisbane midfielder Mitch Robinson yesterday. "Take that out of the game and it's just who is the most talented." God forbid.'

—

Amby sits at the kitchen table shirtless. Where did our young boy go? His shoulders and arms have put on serious bulk from training: he looks big, he looks powerful. I wish he could be bulletproof. When I see the players on TV smashing into each other I flinch and groan.

Meanwhile, in the next room, his older brother, former member of the same footy team, is improvising little French-style waltzes on the piano. He's still in his punk band HateBugs, with all the violent thrashing it entails; the glaring yellow electric guitar always leans beside his bed. But in the dim room where the piano stands against the wall, he gives vent to a stream of enchanting, light-footed, delicate melody.

—

My brother's thirty-three-year-old son chances to drop in just as Amby and I are setting out for Thursday training. My nephew talks about the days when he played footy at school: 'I used to love doing dangerous things. I loved going for speccies. Our coach was also the art teacher. At the end of the season he made a little model of each of the players. Mine,' he says, raising both arms and stretching towards the ceiling, 'was taking a speccy. And right underneath me, he'd put a tiny ambulance.'

I'm going to miss the Colts' first practice match—and the second one too—because, long before I dreamed up this footy thing, I had arranged to go with an old friend to Bendigo to hear Wagner's two-weekends-consuming, industrial-grade opera *Der Ring des Nibelungen*. In these matches, Amby will be playing against two of his close friends who live in other suburbs.

'You're going to miss my Danny game. And my Alex game.'

'I know. I can't believe it. I wouldn't miss them if I didn't have to.'

'It's all right,' he says kindly.

'But it's not all right,' I say, 'not for me.'

In the car on the way to the park I remark that when I saw him at the table without his shirt on I noticed that he has really bulked up.

'Thanks, Helen.'

'I didn't mean it as a compliment. I was just describing it.'

'I don't go round without a shirt to show off my…umm… But sometimes I think I do look…umm…'

He darts me a sly look, and we laugh, zooming down the hill past the new swimming pool, which no one believes will ever be finished.

Sleeveless jumpers with numbers on the back are being spread out on the grass by Harvey's mum. Amby pulls his phone out of his pocket, drops it flat on its back on the damp grass near someone else's bag, and walks away. I have to fight the urge to pick it up and *mind it for him*. I fight it and win.

I haven't been to training in a fortnight. Taking up my position at the boundary rail, in my overalls and straw hat, I'm astounded by how small, young, even weedy the boys look. This impression fades as soon as they begin to work. I love the drills best of all, they're so focused and driven: thirty minutes of fast running and kicking and handball, plunging forward, never hesitating, alert to each other in strange enormous patterns, and hoarsely shouting each other's names. Later, driving home, I tell Amby about my observation. We come up with the explanation that for two weeks I've been watching only AFL matches on TV, where the players are full-grown men, thundering creatures of six foot five with beards and moustaches and massive gym-built arms and legs. 'Of course we look small,' he says.

Here again tonight, hanging over the rail, I see the softness in the faces of these boys, the slenderness, still, of their bodies. How lightly they leap towards the approaching ball, present their chests and bellies to it front-on! When Tommy, the boy with the flying mop of blond curls and the authoritative jawline, puts on one of his bursts of speed, his leg muscles flex as fine as wires under the skin.

Angus, the buzz-cut dude with the big shiny ear stud, seems annoyed that several members of his family have come to watch him train: a sister and small brother, and a man who might be a grandfather. The kids duck under the rail on to the ground and play kick to kick right in front of the goalposts. He shouts at them to stop but they ignore him. He turns away to the other players who are gulping water from their bottles. 'You don't have to *be* here,' he calls back over his shoulder. The man glances at me and we exchange eye rolls. The ball comes to Angus. He kicks for goal and misses, flings himself face-down on the grass.

The U18s saunter up for match sim. Our boys' faces harden and take on a mocking look when they are favoured by the presence of the older team: they stand together looking secretive and mean and defiant, and I spontaneously obey the age-old rule, the lesson women learn from those expressions: the citadel is closed; do not approach.

By 7 pm the whole ground is cooling in shadow. Amby's phone is still lying in the grass. Boys step around it. The sun is low, low, low, and the air beyond the tunnel construction site is dusty with gold. Huge trucks rest in line, one brand new, its silver trims unblemished, its massive crimson flanks still glossy. A crane driver sits in his cabin, bowed over his phone. Why don't they all go home? Isn't the working day over? Trains rattle past on the raised line. A building in the city, way over there behind the hulking masses of the elms, stands glowing like mother-of-pearl in the gentle evening light. I untie my cardigan from around my waist and pull it on.

The coach draws the boys in around him. Their bare legs are stalks, their heads cluster together like flowers. I move in closer to hear what he's saying: he's calling on their co-captain, Jake. The wavy-haired boy steps forward bashfully. The others applaud.

'Come on, Jake,' says Archie. 'Say a few words to your team! Say something about Sunday!'

Jake murmurs, eyes down, 'I hope we win the game.'

On the way home Amby tells me that Jake is always co-captain, every year, because he's the best player on the team. Now I understand the begging cry that goes up from the drills: *JakeJakeJakeJakeJake!*

—

My old friend, with whom I am heading to Bendigo for the *Ring,* is footy mad from childhood. She follows Carlton, knows a thousand times more about the history and terminology of footy than I ever will, yet is prepared to rave with me and put up with my uninformed enthusiasms. When she corrects me I listen with respect. She uses cool expressions like 'junk time', and loves an origin story—for example, the famous Carlton brothers Ed and Charlie Curnow weren't allowed to have PlayStations or hang around inside. They were turfed out by their mother—'she'd lock the door'—to play kick to kick down at the park. By teatime the neighbourhood kids would be worn out, and heading home; but the Curnow boys would play on and on, driven, obsessed, never bored, never running out of energy—'they were like kelpies'.

Saturday is rest night from the *Ring*. We slip away from the restaurants packed with opera buffs, and find a grand old pub where small kids run about in gangs and everyone's in a sociable mood. We order counter meals, and bag a table right in front of the colossal screen. We shout and rage and cheer like everyone around us, invoking the gods of the game and cursing out its evil spirits of vanity, treachery and needless savagery. Everything, including football, is Wagnerian in Bendigo, heart of the goldfields.

—

On Monday morning Amby comes limping into the kitchen.

'I hear you played really well.'

He lowers his eyes but can't help smiling. 'I had to get a massage after the game. I'm still sore.'

'Have you got bruises, or what?'

'You know that backache I used to get, last season? That wouldn't go away? Well, it's come back.'

I put the kettle on for a hot water bottle, hand it to him in its cotton cover. He slides it under his shirt.

'This kid kneed me in the guts. I hope my intestines aren't twisted, or something. Some people told me afterwards I should have got him back. But I'd already smashed him to the ground with my tackle, so...' He doubles up laughing, clutching the hot water bottle to his belly.

'Would everyone in the team be this sore?'

'Amby went in *hard*,' says his dad. 'He went in harder than anyone else.'

His dad says that when he used to play, he was like this after every game, pain all over, but within a couple of days he'd be back to normal. 'Tackling someone,' he says, 'is extremely satisfying. But you have to get to a point where you learn to love *being* tackled. You can curse yourself for being too slow or too unaware or too cocky, but you have to love it. And you have to respect the tackler. It's like with surfing. You have to learn to love the power of the ocean—when it slams you around and ragdolls you if you stuff up a take-off. It's invigorating. It's part of the joy of it. And it makes you try harder next time. If you don't learn to love it you'll always hover round the edges.'

Now all I can think of is injury. I run my eye down the columns of the sports pages. Martin is suffering only hamstring awareness, not a tear. Short has been ruled out with a calf injury. Gun midfield recruit Hopper suffered a knee injury in a nasty incident late in the game. Lynch suffered a cork. *Suffering. Suffer. Suffered.* I've never heard of half these guys, my knowledge barely extends beyond the Western Bulldogs and their calamities, but I flinch and ache for all of them.

'I'm thirty-one,' says Demons' captain Max Gawn. 'I'm sort of getting towards the twilight and to do a third knee would have been pretty devastating…I was quite upset for a bit. I had a little tear in the change room.'

—

Amby is not satisfied with his hair. 'I think I'll go to a barber.'

'But are you going to stick with the mullet?'

'Yeah. For footy.'

'Why does mullet equal footy?'

'Ohhh—because when you run you can feel it flowing, and it makes you feel fast, but it doesn't flop over your face, so sweat doesn't run down.'

—

The Western Bulldogs are looking bad. Everyone's talking about their collapse of morale. The Saints run all over them. How does the guts drop out of a team like this? We sit down faithfully, in our usual positions on couches and floor, secretly arming ourselves against a season of despair, Amby's dad having a breakdown, bitterness filling the air. But then the bastards get up on their hind legs and beat the Brisbane Lions. Watching our new guy Arthur Jones tearing across the ground at the siren and flinging himself into the arms of Jamarra Ugle-Hagan is enough to make us rejoice, whatever might happen next week. We are a team again.

April

Monday night training. Daylight saving ended while I was out of town at the opera. Once more the link between the quality of the light and one's sense of the time is violated. The gears grind; one must adjust. It becomes harder, and irritates me more, with every passing year. Scores of white seagulls are circling above the ground, feeding on invisible insects. The old men, singly and in pairs, who walk very slowly round the ground, cast vague, benevolent smiles towards the milling boys. A woman in business clothes, very straight-backed, her hair up in an elegant do, sails down the Kensington Road footpath on a scooter, grandly surveying the park as she passes on her homeward way. She smiles at me. In fact on this sweet evening every single person who passes me, where I'm leaning against a tree with my notebook and pencil, greets me with a smile and a nod. I wonder what they think I'm doing. Just being an old duck, I suppose, minding my own business. Waiting. With a hat jammed down to my eyebrows and glasses hanging round my neck.

A boy arrives late, steps off his bike and slings it away from him without a glance. It skids on its side across the grass and lies there. He chucks his bag after it and wrenches his shoes off. The supreme carelessness of the way boys dump their things: it always fills me with wonder. More than anything else about them it makes me know that I am a woman.

Archie is already shouting. I can't hear a word he's saying and I don't care. I've come, I'm here, I'm watching. I'm on duty, even if I haven't got a clue what's going on. The boys are yelling and running and kicking in patterns, the air is full of flying balls. I'm falling asleep on my feet. The sky is a dusty, pearly pink. Two rainbow lorikeets go fleeting past me, chirping shrilly. A moon, a few days off full, pale and flat as a slice of cheese, appears above the elms. It must be nearly Easter. My eyes are blurring and I can't concentrate. Evening is falling fast. Am I going blind as well as deaf? A long grey cloud swallows the moon.

A woman wanders up to the rail with a dog: 'Why are they playing in the dark?'

At first I don't recognise her in the thickening dusk: it's Archie's mum. 'I don't know! They should turn on those big klieg lights!'

'Melbourne City Council's supposed to. They've complained, but nothing's been done.'

'Look at that soccer team on the other ground,' I say resentfully, 'which is lit up like Luna Park.'

She shrugs: 'They must have the ear of the king.'

A dozen women in glaring head-torches jog past in a cloud of chatter, and vanish in the gloaming. I can no longer make out the boys, they're only shapes rushing back and forth, though I can hear them gasping and grunting, and the thick whack of boot into leather. They are running madly, blindly, in the dimness. I'm hating this. Someone's going to get hurt. My heart's beating too fast. It's like the opera we saw in Bendigo, *Götterdämmerung*, where the brutal hunters all in black go seething across the stage, a raven soars overhead and Hagen plunges his spear into Siegfried's back.

Just as I'm starting to panic, Archie's clear voice cuts through: 'You can play British Bulldog, or you can go home.'

The boys come panting off the field, jostling, exhilarated. No one's hurt. While they're picking up their things a kid I've never seen before, some blow-in, swings like a sloth from the boundary rail. One of the players says he can't come to training at Easter, he's going to a party.

The dangling stranger says loudly, 'Going to a party, are ya? With a girl? Is she a slut?'

I don't hear an answer.

'You wanna be a gay dog-fucker?' says the dangler.

'*What?*'

'Ya wanna be a gay dog-fucker?'

The object of this turns his back in contempt, buckles his bike helmet and pedals away on to the dark road.

Amby appears to have heard none of it. In the car home he says cheerfully, 'All you want, after training, is either a bowl of hot soup or a big lump of steak.'

—

The family goes down the coast for Easter and I'm home alone. For the first time I wonder if this book is a mistake. Am I wasting my time? Making a fool of myself, trespassing on men's territory, ignorant of their concerns and full of irrelevant observations and thin-skinned responses? I'm losing my nerve. I also know that at about this stage of everything I've ever written or tried to write, I get scared. I know it's part of the deal, that I just have to slog on past it, but knowing this does not help.

On Saturday night I want to watch the Bulldogs play Richmond. It's not on free-to-air. I go next door and try to set it up on their TV, but Kayo keeps enragingly cutting out, so I run home, tune in to ABC774, and crouch breathless over my crackly old transistor for the whole second half. I've never paid full attention to a radio footy broadcast before and I realise what a refined skill it is, this old-fashioned purely oral commentating—to keep up with the play, identify each player by name, account for the umpire's decisions, recognise every strategy, tactic and move, to make us *see* it in all its wild, driving action—'A goal on the run coming outa traffic on his wrong foot!' I am gripped by the game and find that when I hear our players' names I'm able to see them, to imagine their familiar faces and haircuts and bodies and gestures from all the times I've seen them on TV. My visual imagination sharpens as the game goes on. I'm in love with the commentators for their experience and skill, their nasal voices raving on tirelessly, the rising and falling register of their emotions.

After the final siren I sprawl on the couch with a gin and tonic and watch *Im Westen Nichts Neues* on Netflix. I turn it off ten minutes before the end, in the middle of the final bayonet charge that a bunch of exhausted, befouled, maddened, war-destroyed young soldiers are driven to hurl themselves into, on the orders of a hatchet-faced lunatic in a pointy helmet, after the Armistice has been signed and hostilities halted. I can't stand any more. I don't even know why I'm watching it, wrecking the joy of having seen the Bulldogs fight to the end of a close game against Richmond, and win.

——

'In past years,' says Amby, 'I've never really been a tackler—but it feels *soooooo* good to tackle someone. And this year I've become a tackle machine! Well, this is *my* opinion.'

'What feels so good about it?'

'I guess it's basically inflicting physical harm but with no actual hard feelings. It's just *aaaaapchwoooooo* and then you get up and keep playing, and then at the end you shake hands, and no one remembers anything.'

——

In the car on Thursday Amby says, 'I can't wait for you to see a match.'

'Why?'

'Because you'll see how good I am—nah—because it's much more exciting and intense than training. Specially now, because we're *good*. We're really starting to be a team. For years it must have been so boring when people came to our games—you had to watch us get thrashed nearly every time. But now you'll see good play—and *fights*.'

Six pm and someone must have spoken to the king: the big lights on the sky-high poles are on. They're so dazzling that I have to keep my hat on to shield my eyes. Everyone's back from Easter holidays. I settle into my position, leaning against a tree trunk at the western end, near what I think might be the forward pocket. It gets dark so much earlier now.

I'm standing around dreamily in the dusk, listening more than looking. I notice a ball wedged under the outside curve of the skate ramp. I've made a point of never picking up any of the balls that sail over the boundary during the drills. I want to maintain my witness role and not enlist myself as a servant or a fan; and this anonymity is reinforced by the fact that right from the start not a single one of the boys has given me eye contact or even appeared to notice that I exist. I'm always holding a notebook—the badge of my purpose—but I stay well back, even when they gather round Archie near the goals and I'm dying to hear what he's saying to them. He plays along with their serene obliviousness to my existence. This frees me. I'm a phantom in a daggy brown coat and a permanent straw hat. This evening, though, I think that the yellow ball stuck under the skate ramp might not be noticed. So I stroll over and pull it out, and pick up another one off the grass on my way back to the rail. I'm too small to pick up a footy in one hand. This annoys me. I have to stow my notebook in my coat pocket and carry the balls against my chest. Behind the goals I let them fall, clumsily, like a toddler.

It's been a fine day, after a week of grey rain and cold and having the heating on. The air is mild, there's no breeze: a sense of luxury undeserved. My favourite city building looms beyond the row of still-leafy elms, perfectly two-dimensional from here, a slab of silver that draws to itself the remainder of the daylight and holds it in an ethereal mineral glow.

Running drill, back and forth, Archie shouting, counting down from fifteen. I still know hardly any of their names. My failing memory refuses to absorb them. But a few stand out. Many boys run earnestly, with effort, but Tommy puts on a burst of speed without seeming to exert himself. He is fleet-footed, his wiry body weightless, he's always out in front. And his younger brother Ned, so thin and quick, his white-blond hair shining even in the darkest corner of the ground, can duck and twist his way out of anything and emerge with the ball in his hands. I notice Angus because of his earring. He's tall and slim and dreamy, sometimes has to be woken to his duty. Remy is denser, more compact, his dark hair cut in a thick mass on top and radically shaved beneath. He is a commanding figure, terrifically concentrated, always calling for the ball in his ringing voice: they trust him, and look to him.

An old man rambles by, long straggly white hair under his cap, his dark-blue hoodie bears the legend CHEER SQUAD

MEMBER. A runner in shoes many sizes too big for him goes shuffling along. In the western sky above the unseen river, the last soft flush of evening; and as the flush fades, so does the warmth. The sweetness of the dark air, the scent of grass. And always the merciless flashing of the large yellow warning lights on the cranes and diggers working late on the tunnel beside the railway line.

No handball drills today, just the insistent running and, later, 'contest': boys in pairs race side by side, shouldering and shoving and yelling, fighting to mark a ball that a third boy has kicked in their direction. '*Moine. Moine. Moine. Moine,*' they cry. I could watch this all night.

Now they are to verse the U18s, some of whom are wearing bibs in pastel colours. Archie tosses hi-vis bibs at the U16s and they yank them on. It's match sim and it spreads right across the field. Somehow the action is always happening on the far side of the oval. I know from experience that by the time I've trudged all the way round there, to get close enough to see what's going on, the tide of the game will turn and they'll rush to where I was standing before. So I walk halfway round, sit on the curved back of the only bench, and watch in a dream as they struggle in the dimness till it's 7.30 and they're all slowing down and touching hands.

It's over, they tramp back to where they've dumped their gear and it's home time.

Was I bored? No, I couldn't call it boredom, it's too dreamy and pleasant. But I couldn't really say I was thinking.

—

Down in St Kilda, at the Galleon, I have lunch with a jour-
nalist friend from way back. I tell him what I'm writing about.
He says he's been going to the Essendon game with the same
four people every week of every season since he was eleven.

'Great,' I say. 'You can explain to me the changes to the
sub rule.'

'I can,' he replies, sitting up straighter, 'and I will.'

He lays it out for me, crystal clear. At last I understand it. I
go home armed with the sort of facts I am normally bereft of.
By the following morning I can't remember a thing he said.

Blokes I know get excited when I tell them I'm trying to
write about footy. You should do this! You should do that! I'll
take you to the MCG! You should talk to so-and-so! Have you
read this, or that? I think they're imagining the books *they*
would write. Their books would be full of facts and stats and
names and memories. They have been formed by footy. I can't
do it their way. I don't know how. I get panicky. The only
thing I can think of to say is, 'It'll be a nanna's book about
footy.' Short silences fall.

I can tell an arcane footy joke—for example, the one
about the sign on the eastern suburbs church that posed
the challenging moral question: 'What would you do if
Christ came to Hawthorn?' and on which some wag had
spray-painted: 'Move Peter Hudson to centre half-forward.'
Or the Tandberg drawing of a tiny chopper circling over the
city towing a banner that read: 'Jezza out. Go to your homes.'

But I keep to myself the moment in the year 2000 when footy shot its first arrow into my heart.

I had come back to Melbourne after seven years in Sydney, wrung out, single again, a lost soul in the inner west. One night, in my rented house, I saw a doco on TV called *Year of the Dogs*. And it changed my life. It had been made a few years earlier, at a time when the Australian Rules code was being established countrywide. Minor teams were being amalgamated and renamed, shifted to other states, losing their vital links with the working-class Melbourne suburbs they came from. The clubs' supporters were grief-stricken. Frankly, this was of little interest to me. But then the captain of the struggling, impoverished Footscray, a man with a modest manner and a profile off a coin, explained why he had declined an offer from a more famous, more successful club. He said, 'I got a letter from a young boy. "Dear Chris Grant, please don't leave. I haven't got much money. This is all I can give." And he'd sticky-taped on to the letter a fifty-cent piece. So of course I couldn't leave, could I.'

I got off the couch, went straight to the computer with my credit card, and joined his club.

—

At dinner on Thursday night after Amby's training, his big brother, who has been playing chess all afternoon with his friend, is cheerful and forthcoming.

At the table he says, 'This is probably a dumb question,

but—is there anything more than soap that I should be using in the shower? There are so many tubes and little bottles—is there something I'm missing?'

His mum and I reassure him on this point. We kick around a few jokes about women and their 'precious salves and unguents', then follows a discussion about shampoo, whether it's all it's cracked up to be or is actually damaging to one's hair. We compare hair types, problems and advantages.

Meanwhile Amby, upon whose head a large U18 player had heavily landed after a contest an hour ago, sits in silence, exhausted, smeared with mud, not having had time to wash between training and dinner. Every time I see him quiet and pale and sore, sitting at the table with us, eating but in another universe, my heart gives a lurch. Does he have to nerve himself, each time he trains or plays? When I drive him to training I pull up in the street beside the park, and he grabs his bag, leaps out without a word or a backward look, and runs towards the action. I stay in the car for ten minutes, to give him time to arrive alone. Without his grandmother and her anxieties.

—

On Saturday morning at around eight I feed the chooks, and walk into the house next door. No one's in the kitchen, only the dog, who wakes on the couch and gives me a pleading look as he stretches his spine. Mess of butter and crusts on the bench. Amby's room is a bombsite, door wide open. Out the front, their car's missing. Where is everyone? Have I forgotten something, have they gone without me? Or didn't they think to tell me about it? A little rush of desolation. It doesn't matter if I'm not there. No one needs me. I'm not essential after all. I'm only a witness. It's one of the sporadic bursts of reality that grandparents have to bear. You're making a serious mistake if you start to think you're near the centre. You're on the periphery. You're a servant. A hanger-on. And soon you'll be dead.

I make a few calls and find that Amby's working his shift at Cheaper Buy Miles on Racecourse Road. My joie-de-vivre rallies and I set out for the GP clinic to get my flu shot. I am first in the queue! And better still, the middle-aged dude behind me has to pay $45 for his shot, while mine, because I am eighty, is free.

—

Port Adelaide beat the Bulldogs in an honourable game at Adelaide Oval, in rain that falls and falls and falls, in white sheets, in *silvery* sheets, making the ground so slippery that the poor blokes can hardly stay on their feet or keep a grip on the ball.

'A new ball every quarter,' says Amby's dad. 'When it's wet it's like a piece of soap.'

Bontempelli is best on ground. Weightman is back from injury: he takes a fabulous screamer, kicks four goals. He's had an over-thought haircut, some parts shaved, some clenched on top in a bunch, the rest dangling wetly behind. And what's happened to his pretty, youthful looks? He has thickened somehow, in the face—he's hardened. He's fully a man, but still a wonderful little live-wire, eager and strong and super-keen. While waiting he dances lightly from foot to foot.

After the siren Amby leans over with his phone to where I am sitting on the floor and whispers, 'Look at this. Keep looking at his dick.'

It's a tiny video of Weightman, scrambling to his feet after a tackle. His actual dick has got loose from the leg of his shorts. He tucks it back in at lightning speed. We utter muffled snorts of shock and laughter. We all hope that his mortification is soothed by the headlines this morning about his speccy, even if it is a double-entendre: 'Weightman screamer has serious hang time'.

Later, razzed about his wardrobe malfunction, he will reply suavely, 'What I did, I did for my country.'

———

Tonight Amby, his brother, his parents and I walk along beside the railway line to Pho House for dinner. His brother strides between his parents, chattering to them at length, and I bring up the rear with Amby, whose hair his mum has recently snipped into a better shape. He tells me he thinks he's missed his chance 'to get into the League'. I don't hear clearly, he explains and I still don't understand.

'Have you been hoping to play in the AFL?'

'Yes, but I'm not tall enough, and I'm not fast enough, and I'm lazy.'

'Lazy? You don't look lazy to me.'

'I mean I'm not...'

'Obsessed?'

'Yes.'

He doesn't appear to be unhappy about this missed chance, whatever it was. And in my heart a little breath of relief. He won't get hurt.

———

On Thursday my sax-playing sister comes to training with us. She follows Geelong and knows so much more about footy than I do that when she lays down her strictures and theories in fluent argot I am envious and become disheartened. I feel like saying, 'Why don't *you* write this bloody book, smart-arse?' She tells me that before he ran on to the field Amby said to her, 'I haven't trained with this haircut yet.' When we've stopped laughing she reports that his big sister, erstwhile tackle machine of her university team, has told her he's 'a bit vain' as a footballer. But as soon as training starts, the grin is wiped off her face.

'He's *good*,' she says in a faint voice.

And he is—he's strong and keen, his kicking is powerful and well-aimed, and everything he does looks serious and confident.

While we watch she tells me what happened at the airport

when the band she plays in was in the rat race at security. Everyone in the world was heading to Adelaide for the AFL's so-called 'Gather Round', and she recognised the guy next to her as Jamarra Ugle-Hagan. 'He had plugs in his ears, and he was keeping his face down over his phone. He's huge! I'd thought he was small, like Eddie Betts—but he must be over six foot tall.'

Further up the line, she says, there were more of the Bulldogs. The sound guy from her band, a Dogs supporter, reported to her that Bont in particular was being charming and sociable with strangers, agreeing to selfies, and putting everyone in the line into a good mood. 'I think they should have AFL players in every airline queue,' she says, 'to spread patience and general good humour throughout the land.'

Archie's dad wanders up with their dog and stands beside us at the rail. He tells us that trainers have to be qualified in first aid.

'Most trainers are parent volunteers,' he says. 'Even at this level of football you can't start a match until two registered trainers are in attendance, with their bags—whereas at training itself nobody has to be there. The coach is on his own. Imagine what could happen—here in the dark, for example.'

Right on cue the tall lights pop on. While I'm listening to Archie's dad I'm turned away from the ground, but his eyes stay on the play.

'Did you see that?' he says. 'What Arch just did? He kicked a torp—a beautiful torp—the sort that every player wants to kick. The boys stopped playing and watched it sail overhead.'

He mimes rapt, open-mouthed gazing. 'He'll only do one.' He laughs. 'Just the one. And they'll remember it.'

—

The Bulldogs thrash Fremantle. I don't know how, because we keep missing goals. A shockingly fast and furious game. The sort where I quail on the floor with my arms around my head. When a couple of great lumps of Dockers rough up Caleb Daniel, Amby's father bellows, 'Ya fuckin' big dickheads!'

—

An hour before we leave for Amby's first real match of the season, I'm scraping shit out of the chooks' roosting box and notice him bent over, studying something on the bricks near the clothesline.

'What is it?'

'A wasp and a bee, fighting.'

I approach. The wasp flies away. We remain bent. I confess that I wouldn't know a wasp from a hole in the ground.

'They're more brightly coloured than bees.'

The wasp, on its erratic flight path, returns to the scene of the crime. We bend lower.

'Oh yes. I can see its stripes. Sheet, it's really murdering that bee.'

The bee is moving feebly, trying to wriggle away, but the wasp is heavier and stronger, violently in command.

'Is that what it's like to get tackled?'

'*No*,' he says. 'It's *not* like getting stung to death.'

—

On the drive west to Sunshine for the game, Amby in the back seat is silent and rather pale—tall and powerful, broad shoulders, long bare legs. Many of the houses we pass, with their pastel asbestos walls, messy yards and gateless entries, feel familiar to me. 'I like it out here. It reminds me of Ocean Grove.' It's 'the past' that it's reminding me of, my childhood, the 1940s and 50s. At a railway crossing we pause beside a deserted house that's partly obscured by a sign advertising the large, grey apartments that will be built on its site. The side of the doomed house is painfully appealing to me. Shrubbery presses close to its window, old bricks lie about, a rusty barrel; its driveway is tyre-flattened mud with traces of green. What am I doing out here? What will I say if someone asks me? 'I'm with the Colts. I'm their witness.'

And here they are, the Colts U16s, playing a constricted kick to kick in a small concrete yard beside the Sunshine clubhouse, all in their team jumpers, clean and ready, their hair shampooed, their faces shining but purposefully blank. I am not used to seeing them in full daylight. How young they look, how smooth, unlined! They have men's voices but boys' faces. Xavier has cut off his low ponytail. Aiden's long mullet flows down the back of his neck in a glistening curve, as if blow-dried. Archie strides up to them with a folder against his chest, his cap on backwards, white-cheeked but smiling.

I find a space on the boundary fence, near a woman with a tiny black poodle on an extendable lead. Small boys pass in pairs, always one holding a ball, their heads together in solemn conference. The oval is in good nick; it's got that slightly domed shape that makes you feel you can see the curve of the planet.

I hear a burst of cleats on the concrete behind me and turn in time to see the Colts form a line and stride towards the ground. Our boys. My God, they are men, in their vertical stripes and white shorts, even the little skinny ones are men: it's the groupness of them that makes them men, moving with purpose in a thick bloc. Why do I feel like crying?

The siren, the bounce, boys explode in all directions and I'm lost. Amby's dad is standing near me, following with his experienced gaze, making comments, letting out the odd cheer or groan, but I'm in a panic. The ground is too enormous, I'm too small, my eyes are no good, I can't recognise anyone or understand what's happening. I need TV, give me TV—the edited and packaged version of the match with its roving cameras and close-ups and aerial shots, and commentators pouring out names and manoeuvres and opinions, the voices that know everything—I am totally dependent on them.

Oh it's hopeless, and I can't pretend that my eye is not always seeking out Amby. I try to force myself to survey the game in a detached spirit, but I know the shape of his shoulders, the angle of his run, and there he goes, breaking out of a pack, holding the ball forward and low, running in long strides, getting his boot to it and sending it sailing down the wing.

At quarter time I slink out on to the ground behind Archie. I want to hear his commanding voice, someone to pull it together for me, the spectacle of what the hell I've been straining to see. The boys, panting, press shoulder to shoulder before him. Amby is right at the back. His face shocks me, darkly flushed, open-mouthed, glistening with sweat: what I see is *a man*.

'If you take a mark,' says Archie, 'don't just bomb it in! They'll mark it! That's what they *want* us to do! Let's have a bit of composure! Take your time!'

Angus, minus his earring, is standing to the right of the coach and behind him, looking into the distance—is he even listening? 'Come in front, Angus—come in front.' The boy obeys, reluctantly. Is something biting him?

Archie's clear, strong voice: 'Tackling—there's too much of this *patting*!' He mimics it, whacking his flat palms pointlessly all over the nearest boy's chest and shoulders. 'You've got to go for their *hips*! And bring 'em down! Also, I see people *walking*! Are *they* walking? If I see anyone walking with their head down, sad because they didn't get a goal—that's bullshit! *Never be walking*! We're five goals down but we can win this! We're a better team than they are. They're winning because they're working harder.'

They are?

The siren sounds and I try to watch analytically instead of gazing in a trance. And Archie's right. Sunshine are going harder, they're heavier and faster and more determined in the contests. Some of the Colts seem to me to be holding back at crucial moments. Are they scared? Of getting hurt? Who wouldn't be?

'At least compete,' mutters Amby's dad. 'We're not competing in the air—we're not flying with any conviction for the ball!'

Archie turns away from the field with a pant of frustration, pressing his fists into his eyes. They're all over us, kicking goal after goal. And yet some of the Colts, even I can see, keep throwing themselves into it with everything they've got. They get the ball up to our forward line and that's where it all falls apart. I dimly grasp that this is why we're losing; and after the final siren it's what everyone around me is saying, so maybe I'm not as clueless as I think.

Amby in the car home is given the front passenger seat, the place of honour. He is very quiet. He has a six-inch bloody graze on each elbow. His dad praises his playing. The praise is sincere, and deserved: he played bravely, and skilfully, he didn't let up. They begin to analyse the game, side by side in the front. I lean forward but the radio is on loud, tuned to another game, and drowns out what they're saying. I feel old and deaf and awed, in the back seat with the dog.

The next night, after dinner, the table strewn with picked bones, Amby's dad comes out with memories of his own youthful footy years. They compare notes on tagging.

'One time,' he says, 'this bloke was tagging me and he kept pinching me, you know? How they get at this bit of skin round your waist? And pinch you?'

What? They *pinch* you? Isn't pinching sort of girly? Is it allowed?

'And finally,' he says, 'I just lost it. I swung my arm right round, like *this*, and I smashed him. And then I smashed him again. I was reported. But he never pinched me after that. Don't get me wrong—I'm not in favour of violence, but—'

Amby leans forward: 'But I feel like that all the time. And I don't just mean in footy, either. I really want to—' He grits his teeth, thrusts out both arms and mimes punching and throttling.

We're all laughing, but nervously. I suppose they'd talk differently if I wasn't here.

—

At training on Monday I feel a bit off. Probably a cold coming on.

Archie takes the rap for the loss. He says to me, 'I think I was out-coached. He'd been coaching those kids since they were eight. I've only had these guys for a couple of months.'

Away they go, faithfully through their drills. Kicking and marking—I love how they leap to meet the approaching ball, to get it on to their chest. I have become aware of a boy called Boof. He's quite chunky, short-legged, with a low centre of gravity, not a classic AFL physique. He has a fine Mediterranean nose, tight dark curls and, like Remy, a carrying voice and a presence. Boys seem keen to be noticed by him.

Archie's dad has come tonight, partly to watch his daughter training with the girls' footy team she coaches: 'A lot of the girls come from netball. You ask them what they like best about footy and they say, "Tackling. I *love* tackling!"'

I ask him why Angus was vaguing out during yesterday's match.

'I don't know. Arch thinks Angus is a really good player. He's tall and fast and strong, but he tends to lose concentration. Sometimes he'll just wander off, and stand over there, on his own. When Amby's dad and I played, everyone was treated the same. These days the coach has got to manage them. And Arch—well, he's smart, but he's only twenty.'

—

I don't feel so good. I can't smell or taste anything. I do a RAT. Oh hell. I'm vaccinated to the eyeballs but I've caught it. Half a dozen warning calls come from people who were at that bloody art opening last week. Apparently you don't have to isolate any more but I'm going to stay home. I've got some anti-virals, I've heard they knock it over fast.

On Saturday, home on my own, I resort again to my transistor. Dogs versus Hawks on 3AW. I don't know a single Hawthorn player, but the Bulldogs, as the commentators shout their names, emerge one by one from the radio's black and white into the glory of their ethereal blue. The commentators must be old—what young dude would shout, '*Hooooooooo!* Bailey Smith! Rapunzel! He's let down his hair!' In that moment I give in to daggy old radio and its time-honoured power to entertain and serve—and I flash on a life-size sculpture I once saw in the courtyard of the FDR Museum in

Washington DC: a little table with a wireless standing on it, and a man in rough working clothes hunched forward on a kitchen chair, chin in hand, listening in rapt concentration to the voice of President Roosevelt.

The others have gone to the game at Marvel Stadium, so I shout and scream by myself while an eighteenth birthday party rages rhythmically a few doors up the street. At quarter time the scores are almost level. By the final siren we've won by twenty-nine points, and the Bulldogs are 'back in the conversation', as the commentators put it, in the adventurous tone of old farts trying out a hip expression.

Later I mask up and go next door, where I find Amby and his dad home from the ground, still in their Bulldogs colours, absorbed in the replay. On the big screen as I walk into their kitchen I see the mighty figure of Bontempelli in flight, an archangel out of Blake or Milton, all crystalline and celestial—and the *blue* of the Bulldogs jumper! So intense, so mouth-watering, so made of sky.

—

Sunday. I'm testing negative. I turn up at our park nice and early, for the Colts' game. It's the freshest, sunniest, loveliest mid-autumn afternoon. We're versing Werribee Centrals. The junior teams are still playing. As I drift round the oval a crestfallen lad of ten or so hobbles past me towards the street, leaning his weight across his mother's shoulders. A trainer walking beside them says, 'Call the clinic. Tell them you're coming. If you go straight to Emergency you'll sit there for six hours.'

I like watching the younger kids. They're slower and I can sometimes read what they're doing, or trying to do. Near the end of their game I get my first ever close view of what I think must be shepherding: a boy thrusts out both arms in a T and turns his back on the boys thundering down on his teammate who's got the ball. He stands four-square, leaning back against the oncoming tacklers, and holds them at bay by sheer strength and determination—like a levee holding back a flood. I let out a cheer.

Out run the U16s: the dry, oddly muffled pattering sound of studs on concrete, like the first burst of a hard rain shower. Their match is difficult, as always, for me to see and follow, all those numbered specks racing round on the far side of the oval, but every now and then I get a fix on Amby. He is in the ruck today and I can't believe how high he can leap to tap the ball down from the bounce.

No sooner is the third quarter rolling than the game is stopped for a head count. What? They've got one more player on the field than we have. One of the Werribee team runs back to the boundary. Before the uneven numbers were noticed, Werribee had kicked three goals.

'Used to be,' says Amby's dad, 'if you were found to have an extra player they'd wipe your score. Now, I don't know.'

Just before the three-quarter-time siren, when the Colts are ahead by a healthy margin, Amby gets a free within reach of goal. He lines it up and gets his boot to it, and while all eyes are on the ball's trajectory, the siren goes, the kick falls short—and down in the goal square, twenty metres along the boundary fence from where Amby's dad and I are standing, *something happens.* All hell breaks loose and twenty boys are wrestling and shoving and tearing at jumpers, wrenching at each other by the shoulders and upper arms, rolling on the ground trying to squash and choke each other. It's so total and so wild that that the spectators stand frozen. The umpires are invisible, their whistles peeping feebly.

A woman behind me says, 'They're so full of testosterone—I don't know how they expect them to teeter on the brink—they get praised for playing hard and then when they go over the edge nobody knows what to do!' People with some sort of authority burst out from each team's small group of supporters and break it up.

While peace is being imposed, the Werribee players roar in a chorus, 'Number four! Four! Four!'—our wingman, Meth, long-legged, fearless and fast, with a mullet of dark curls and an ironic grin, who has probably never broken a rule in his life. The umpire points at him and away he trots, with a shrug, carrying the sins of his team.

After the final siren we rush to the rooms to hear what happened. Amby says in an injured tone, 'I didn't see it! *I* was the bloke trying for the torp!' The boys, filthy and dishevelled, yell their victory song, and Archie says, 'About what happened—we saw it was one of them who started it—their big guy—a team will do that when they're losing—and good on you, Josh, for backing your teammate when he was hit—I was pleased with the way you all handled it. We'll talk about it at training tomorrow.'

—

An important-looking club email arrives for Amby's mum: '… the worst behaviour I could ever have imagined at junior sport from an opposition spectator. I feel sick to have witnessed it. We will not accept this behaviour and will ensure that this person is punished to the fullest extent.'

What on earth, who on earth, can it have been?

—

Monday morning I go into their kitchen to deliver the one egg the chooks have managed. Amby is at the bench making himself a ham, cheese and tomato roll for school lunch.

'How'd you pull up?'

'Not good.'

'Sore all over?'

'Worse. Really sore here'—pointing at the right side of his chest—'and the same place in the back.'

'What happened?'

'This kid tackled me. He grabbed me like a hug from the back and threw me down. I had a hot bath last night but it didn't help.'

'Do you think something's broken?'

'No.'

'Are there bruises?'

'No.'

'There's probably bruising inside.'

What would I know?

Working slowly, trying to cut a piece of cheese off the block, he slices his fingertip. '*Look*,' he says bitterly.

'Is it bleeding? Go and wash it. I'll finish your roll.'

'Make it so the tomato won't soak through,' he says from the doorway. 'Put the tomato *between* the cheese and the ham.'

'Will I put lettuce in? To act as a barrier?'

'Okay.'

He returns with a white bandaid on the very tip of his finger. 'It looks silly.'

'Put a second one on, around the tip, to hold the first one on.'

'You've got that roll upside down,' he says. 'Turn it over. Wrap it in this stuff.'

'Tell me about the brawl.'

'Right. Well, I didn't actually see anything, because I had my free kick, but I heard that one of their players pushed one of ours. Josh pushed him back, there was a bit of push and shove, and then a woman dressed in black came running on to the ground, and she hit someone, and that's when everyone started fighting, and she'll never be allowed to come to any more games.'

'My God.'

'And,' he says, folding his lunch bag and stowing it in his backpack, 'Silas spat on someone.'

'Spat?'

'Yep.'

'I am definitely coming to training tonight.'

—

Texts. 'Hey Archie can I come in closer tonight when you talk to the boys about what happened yesterday?'

'Of course. There's a few things to talk about. One of our boys has been suspended and next week we play Newport who are very well known for getting into a bit of argy bargy so will be important that we don't engage in it.'

—

In next door's kitchen, before training, I tell Amby and his dad that someone's been reported: 'It couldn't be Meth, could it? What did Meth do?'

Boy and man bellow in chorus: *'NOTHING!'*

'When there's been a brawl,' says Amby's dad, 'the umpire has to send off one player from each team. The Werribee guys all yelled "Four! Four! Four!" So he sends number four off, and that's Meth.'

'But why did they pick on Meth?'

'BECAUSE HE WAS PLAYING SO WELL!'

In the car I ask Amby if Archie will start the talk right away.

'No. He'll let us warm up first.'

'I feel upset. Do you?'

'No. Not really.'

'I mean—my heart rate's up. I'm not just an observer any more. I'm realising that I care about the team. That I'm involved.'

He looks out the window at the traffic. 'It's the stage we're at. We're all full of hormones. Some guys are men. They've got beards.'

———

A few more parents than usual have come tonight. Nobody is mentioning 'the brawl'. People ask each other, with delicacy, 'Were you at the game? Did you see the incident?' The question gives strangers a way to launch real conversation.

Harvey's mum tells me that one of her sons, reporting the scapegoating of innocent Meth, said, (she mimics his low, knowing tone) 'That was *racist*, Mum. They sent off *the only brown one*.' She laughs. 'And I said to him, "Don't jump to conclusions. They needed to get rid of Meth because he was playing so well."'

Leaning on the rail near me is a friendly-looking guy who always wears a felt hat. He's Joey's dad, an art historian. He too admits to being upset by the incident, which he not only witnessed but filmed.

'You've got *vision*?'

'Yes! I was filming it on my phone, and a big guy from the other team's supporters came charging up and told me to stop. He said, "You're not allowed to film this! Stop filming! Delete it! Right now!" I didn't know if I was allowed to or not. I even thought maybe I should delete it. But when I went home and told my wife—she's a criminal barrister—she said, "Oh, that's *ridiculous*. Of course you were allowed to film—it's a public place!'"

We both start to laugh and can't stop, hanging on to the metal rail in helpless paroxysms.

Myths are already forming around the incident. A personage called 'the woman in black' is said to have barged into the goal square where the first blow had been struck by one of the Werribee players. In black? Do they mean a dark jacket? Was she in hijab? I still can't find out what she is actually supposed to have done. Even Joey's dad, the filmer, can't seem to answer that question. I suppose I could investigate, but something makes me want to stay in this cloud of unknowing. Some call her the woman in black, some say no! I saw her, she had red hair! Others say she was definitely a blonde. Xavier's dad, the trainer and assistant coach, joins us at the rail. I suggest to him that the woman in black might be a figment.

'No,' he says. 'If there are various reports, it proves it's true. Where there's smoke there's fire.' He is concerned that people might get the idea that the mysterious woman was his wife, who went on to the field to defend one of our players, Antonio, into whose throat a Werribee player was heavily pressing the point of his elbow. 'Poor Antonio! He might well be completely traumatised—he might have PTSD! Or even decide to give up the sport!'

While the grown-ups are having these whispered conversations, the boys are throwing themselves into their drills with rowdy keenness. They seem very revved up, shouting a lot in hoarse voices. They couldn't give a shit about the incident. It's in the past and they just want to play.

They work for twenty minutes, then Archie calls in three of the senior boys, Boof, Remy and Josh. I don't know what makes them senior, they just are. They look mature, calm and solid; they have natural authority. I move closer. He is warning them in a low voice about this Sunday: 'Newport,' he says, 'have a reputation for roughness and fighting.' He's asking them to make sure that our players don't retaliate. As usual, the boys, even though I'm standing right beside them, pay me absolutely no attention. This is not impolite. In their consciousness I simply do not exist. But non-existence grants me full freedom and I listen blatantly, taking notes.

Soon Archie calls out to the others: 'Come in, boys. Come in.'

They jog to him and stand facing him in a close ring.

He knows their attention span, and keeps it short and simple. 'Okay. I know they instigated it and finished it, and I get that you stick up for your mate, but it's not good enough. One of our players did something he shouldn't have, and he got reported. So, he can't play for two weeks and that's bad— he's one of our best players.'

Everyone must know what Silas actually did, but nobody mentions it.

'During the time when they had nineteen players on the

ground and we had only eighteen,' Archie goes on, 'they kicked three goals. That part of their score will be wiped.'

The boys raise their eyes from the grass and glance at each other. A thrill runs through them. They tighten their lips. Someone whispers, 'Wow.'

'This week,' Archie goes on, 'we're playing Newport. Every single time I've played Newport there's been a fight. So we have to prepare ourselves for that. If they start it, we don't get into it, all right?'

They murmur, and nod.

Then he calls the boy who spat to come forward and stand beside him: 'Come on, Silas. Speak to your team.'

The strong, dark-haired boy shambles up, pale-faced, grinning awkwardly. He speaks with many pauses. 'I. Did something I. Shouldn't have. Yeah. Bad choice. Let the team down. Sorry guys. I can't play. Yeah. Sorry.' He raises his face, brightens. 'But I'll be there! Supportin' you!'

He looks helplessly at his coach. Archie nods, releasing him. Silas stumps back to the group. It opens to absorb him.

May

In the car on Thursday Amby says, 'My knee's sore. And I know what it is. It's not an injury. I'm having another growth spurt.'

Now that dark falls early, the custom of the pleasant evening stroll is over. Almost the only people who pass me are the women runners with their whirling ponytails and cold-beamed little head-torches. Some of them are wiry and fleet, with the smooth, economical movements of marathon runners; others are plump, with big hips, bellies and breasts; I'm always impressed to see how many of the heavy ones pass me again and again, at a steady pace and breathing easily, able to converse freely with their companions. A chubby man walking slowly is overtaken by the squad. 'You're surrounded by women!' calls one of them. He flaps his hands with a sweet goofy smile: 'Normally that's the ideal thing, but not right now.'

Thick clouds, the cold coming in. Not everyone seems to be here. No Boof, no Remy, none of the other seniors. I take my spot near where they're dumping their bags and pulling on their boots. Someone says, 'I kicked the best goal of my life. And nobody saw it.'

At 6.05 two boys jump out of a car and hurry to the group. 'Thanks for coming, boys,' says Archie with a light touch of sarcasm. They start their drills.

'Stab kicks,' shouts Archie. 'Change the bloke at the front. Change the bloke at the *front*. What the hell was *that*, Harvey?'

I lean on the rail and go off into my trance. The cold air smells of cut grass. I love the old-fashioned lamps that stud the paths, so pale and pretty: they remind me of the ones in *The Lion, the Witch and the Wardrobe*. A full moon drifts out of the clouds—I didn't know it was there!—and withdraws again. Above the row of elms the top halves of city towers float, their outlines obscured by night; the towers *are* night now, columns of it, each one with its coronet of blinking red dots.

Am I bored? It's like sitting in a court watching a trial. There are long passages without drama, but because you're in love with the story and its characters, even the boring parts are interesting. I'm watching footy. Just standing around in a dream, in the presence of footy. And boys. Nameless boys at dusk. In the presence of boys hovering on the verge of manhood.

Joey's dad turns up in a beanie. Three fathers and I stand at the rail, vaguely watching the boys versing the U18s in the dark. I can see Amby is limping, just a slight favouring, but he is refusing to slow down, and flies for the ball, taps it, stoops to it, shoulders out of a pack, kicks with authority. When they shout to each other I try again, and fail, to fix names to bodies.

The play surges to the other side of the ground where, small and dainty as stick figures, the players run back and forth in a frieze along the lit fence of the tunnel construction site.

'They look like that Indonesian puppet play,' says Joey's dad. 'Wayang.'

Another bloke, smiling, open-faced, bounds up the slope from the street and joins us. He looks at me expectantly and puts out his hand. He raises the matter of 'the incident'. We all reply mechanically: the drama has gone out of it now; everyone has calmed down and started to forget it. But he presses it, mentions the fact that the boy who spat has had to make an apology: 'I wonder what he said?'

'I was there. I heard him.'

'You heard him? What did he say?'

I launch an account, mimicking the boy's shy posture and awkward utterance, but two sentences in I twig from the man's eager attention that he must be Silas's dad. I double down on the touchingness of his speech—'Sorry guys. I let the team down'—and take the liberty of adding a grace note: 'They listened to him with *affection*, I thought.'

His dad gives a burst of rather emotional laughter and seizes my hand again. 'Thanks! Thanks for telling me that! I'm so glad you told me! I couldn't get a word out of *him*!'

The other fathers turn to him and laugh, ruefully.

—

Saturday. Covid hits me a second time. So much for anti-virals. I lie in bed all day rereading James Button's marvellous book *Comeback: the Fall and Rise of Geelong.* He interviews former players on the subject of their great coach Malcolm Blight. 'Blight told them to lace their boots on the side, because a knot on the front of the boot might cause a mis-kick. A tackler should drop his knees for balance. Train in proper football gear—no singlets. Socks reveal morale, so keep them up. "Blight," says a former Cat, "was the first coach who taught us how to play. The coaches of the 80s didn't teach blokes how to play footy. They told us why we should win. They'd give the traditional rev-up—we hate these pricks, they've beaten us the last three games…None of that makes you a better footballer. Blight would say, "This bloke's a left-footer, force him to the boundary. This guy will not punch—he'll try to mark so it won't fall far. This guy never takes an overhead mark, so force him under the ball."'

I remember the doco that made me love the Bulldogs: the haranguing coach in the rooms, the soaked and sweating players shamed and bowing their heads. Blight tells Button about having rebuked a player: "'You've cost us the season": in hindsight it sounds bloody stupid and it probably was. But I'd had it said to me many times. There is a thing called coach-speak. If you haven't done it I don't reckon you can understand it. Things come out because of the intensity of the moment, the desire to win.'

—

Saturday night and on TV I flip back and forth between the
Western Bulldogs v Greater Western Sydney on 7 and the
coronation of Charles III on the ABC. I'm struck by the static
quality of the coronation, despite the glorious choral music.
Something deadened, frozen, in all its golden extravagance:
the poor old king, pale and dry-skinned, already wearied by
life, his hands puffy and stiff, his strange silver-buckled shoes,
the Supertunica, the colossal, ridiculous crown being jiggled
and screwed into position on his head; while on a football
field in Canberra, down here on the other side of the world,
thirty-six men in their own formal costumes are running,
skidding, leaping, kicking—rain comes down in misty sheets
and makes them lose their footing—they slide and fall and
pick themselves up and run on.

What's the connection between these rituals? *Is* there a
connection? It entrances me: the doddering, hypnotic slowness
of the jewel-encrusted transfer of power juxtaposed against
the driven, desperate night-ballet of the footballers in the rain.
I turn off the sound, and a Covid-lockdown memory rushes
back: matches played for television before empty stands. In
that solemn silence we could hear the players shouting to
each other, the deep, satisfying thud of boot into ball. It was
a purer version of the game, and we watched it rapt, as if
all the troubles in the world were being boiled down and
redeemed by these complex patterns, these arcane rules and
classic postures of dejection and triumph. Virgil and Homer
would recognise these hulking airborne men: not just their
wildness—*a madman in a four-horse chariot*—but also their

manly tenderness to the wounded—*bracing the captain, arm around his waist, he helped him towards his shelter.*

—

The Bulldogs win. Cody Weightman and Artie Jones are called to the mike. Two ecstatic faces, wide open with laughter, filling the screen with eyes and teeth. (Memory: Amby's brother at five running in from his first day at primary school: 'I made two friends! A white one and a brown one!') These two are famous for sharing a flat since Artie came to town. The interviewer, unable to hide his own exhilaration, says, 'And what do you cook? What's your favourite dish?' Pause. They flash a glance at each other. I'm imagining pies, takeaway, fish and chips. Then Artie says, 'Tortellini. Yeah. Tortellini...*carbonara.*'

—

Stuck at home with Covid. Lying under the doona, reading, dozing, reading again, forgetting everything I've read. After two weeks I emerge negative and drive to the cafe, pick up the *Age*, turn to the sports pages. A photo: Buddy Franklin leaving the field with his arm across the shoulders of a teammate, after Sunday's match, which his team, the Sydney Swans, has lost to Collingwood. Collingwood is at the top of the ladder, Swans at eleven. And the Collingwood crowd booed Buddy Franklin, a hero of the game, a dancing *god* of the game, in his last season. Franklin is thirty-six, battle-hardened. His face, in this photo, is calm, composed; but it is also as soft as a boy's. It's a wounded face, with that wiped look of someone who's copped a ringing slap across the cheek: all his expression lines are gone. In my fortnight of isolation I must have lost a couple of skins: I shock myself by bursting into tears. I turn a page and find 'a Collingwood member' who says he did boo but realises in hindsight that it was 'a mistake': 'I booed,' he said, 'because everyone else booed.' The *Guardian* doesn't hold back: 'It's about the internalised hatred that men—who are the dominant force in shaping and sustaining AFL culture— have for themselves and each other. The Great Southern and Ponsford Stands merely provide a haven for the boozed-up, brittle and broken to project their own self-hatred and inse-curities on to others.'

—

Thursday, on the way to training.

'I still haven't heard about the game I missed.'

'Okay. Because of the pain all down my leg I told Archie I wouldn't be able to go hard, so he kept me on full-back and full-forward. It was *horrible*. I was so *cold*. I only touched the ball twice. I was on this *huuuuuge* guy.'

'But you kicked a goal, didn't you?'

'Yes, but I didn't get any of my anger out. And the goal wasn't very…*nice*.'

'You mean it wasn't sort of heroic?'

'No.'

'But nevertheless it *was* a goal?'

He shrugs, and runs off.

Silas's dad is here tonight. He edges up to me at the rail: 'Hey. The president called me. He gave me some facts. The woman in black tried to punch my lad in the face.'

'Crikey. Did you see the video?'

'He offered to show it to me but I didn't want to see it. The club was prepared to get the cops involved. Charge her with assault. Or make a formal complaint to the league. But Silas's mum and I agreed to let the club handle it themselves. They've banned her from any future Flemington games.'

'And the spit?'

'They said they'd settle for a suspension: apologise and fess you fucked up, and you're water boy for two weeks. We accepted that.'

'Wow. That's really good crisis management.'

I don't know him well enough to go further and say: 'Good on you. That is exemplary parenting.' But that's what I'm thinking.

Boof rides up, slings his bike across the grass. He's wearing trackpants whose crutch is almost at knee level. He jogs between the goalposts and gives one of them a flying kick, making its metal jangle and chime. It's a perfect dark clear evening. Archie makes them warm up by playing soccer. A lot of fancy dancing, twirling kicks behind the shoulder, coarse howls. The boys form a loose ring around a bloke in dark clothes who appears to be demonstrating certain moves and postures. He rolls the footy along the ground for them to pick up: 'Both hands. Both hands!'

Archie's dad tells me the guy is a physio who's teaching them how to change direction without getting injured: how to sidestep.

'Most of these boys have never done a sidestep in their life. They get the ball and all they wanna do is kick it.' He notices Amby's limp. 'There's no doubt you carry injuries, as a footballer. Archie's complaining about his thumb. I say, "Face it. It's gonna hurt for a whole season."'

Archie's dad is one of those invaluable fathers who, along with his wife, is deeply and benevolently sunk into the social fabric of the suburb. He's on the council of the local high school, on the committee of the cricket club and the footy club, you name it. I'm always glad to see him coming: he is a fount of information and gossip, full of energy and ready to laugh; but he has a permanently buggered knee, from too many footy injuries.

On the field Amby, despite his limp, is going hard, running, roaring out names, making commanding gestures. At the boundary rail a father I don't know, in a grey hoodie, is holding forth to Joey's dad about the low standard of umpiring in suburban cricket. He's got a thing about it: he's on a roll. I don't know anything about cricket, so I keep watching the boys play. Archie's dad asks me if I saw 'the brawl'. He remarks that Angus, 'a hothead', did not get involved—that Archie was surprised and very pleased with him for keeping out of it.

Archie calls time. The boys pull their backpacks on and whack the soles of their boots together, to get the mud out. Boof picks up his bike and is dismayed to find that its chain has snapped. The dad in the hoodie forgets about cricket, and turns at once to help him. He bends with the boy over the greasy broken metal. His voice softens, and he says kindly, 'Ah—you're missing a whole link, aren't you.'

—

On Saturday night the Bulldogs are playing Carlton. I rush in from the Queenscliff writers' festival a few minutes after the bounce. I don't think I'll last the distance; I'm spent. Amby's dad has gone to the game on his own. His sister and brother aren't interested. So Amby, his mum and I are the faithful ones at home. In the third quarter I doze off for a moment. When I come to, Carlton have kicked another goal. Oh no, don't tell me the Bulldogs are going to turn on one of their famous collapses—but I start to see what footy journos mean when they talk about Carlton self-sabotaging. They are terrific players. Their skill levels are high, they're fast and strong, there's beautiful play, but some vital coalescing factor is missing—what *is* it? If their kicking had been more accurate early on we would now be in the shit. My heart aches for them—they're such a likeable team, no brutes that I can see and all that dark-haired youthful beauty, their elegant South Yarra haircuts—and I love the generous feeling that flows between them and the victorious Bulldogs after the siren:

some shake hands, some embrace, some laugh. I wonder what they're saying. They seem to like and respect each other. It's been an honourable match. At these sportsmanlike moments I love the game and admire the players without reservation.

—

Sunday. On the drive west to Penleigh Essendon Grammar School in Keilor, Amby's dad talks about the 'gravitas' of Bulldogs players Jamarra Ugle-Hagan and Tim English.

'There's a turning point in your application to any sport, or art—when you want to be really good. And you want to be *thought of* as good. As a good player.'

Amby pays attention but doesn't speak. His dad is so busy philosophising that he misses the exit ramp off the Calder and has to execute a three-kilometre U-turn.

A sparse crowd. Amby's other grandparents have come: his granny, mother of seven, says, 'Amby's one of the last of our boys still playing footy.' It's a splendid ground overlooking the valley of the Maribyrnong River: the smooth, thick turf of a western suburbs private-school sports oval. Under a flight path. Every ten minutes a shining speck materialises in the empty sky and comes floating towards us, wheels down, passing over at such a leisurely speed that we hunch our shoulders, hardly trusting it to remain airborne. Amby's granny counts off the airlines on her fingers: Jetstar, Rex (with propellors whirring), Air New Zealand, and Virgin Virgin Virgin. And Sri Lankan. The boys do not seem distracted by the roaring aerial parade. They dig right in and blaze away.

It's a beautiful day, clear sky, a mild little breeze that puffs from time to time. Families sit on the dense dry grass. You can get a hot dog, with or without cheese. They take cards or cash. I offer cash and fumble it: since Covid I've lost the ability to do a quick sum. There's an unusual quality in the light today, a freshness, a clarity. Or are my eyes working better? I can make out numbers on the players' backs; I even manage, if fleetingly, to translate a few of them into names. We win.

At dinner time Amby, in a singlet that shows his arms and shoulders to advantage, tells us in a casual tone that he's just had a text informing him that the umpires voted him 'number 2 best on ground' in his team. We cheer. He goes on nonchalantly chewing and swallowing. After the meal he asks his brother and me if we want to see the photos of the game that their mum took with her telephoto lens. We move the cat off the swivel chair and lean over the desktop. The photos are wide shots, five or six players in each, and every boy is caught at a moment of distorting strain: mouth twisted, jaw clenched, legs stretched, arms grabbing and shoving and wrenching, feet springing off the ground or pressing into it on unbelievable angles of balance and turn.

'Don't you get scared?'

Amby shrugs. 'At the beginning of every year you're scared. You're with new players and you have to prove your worth. But once you've started, it all comes back to you, and you say to yourself, "I'm a good player, I'm strong, I'm not going to get hurt."'

'When I played for the Colts,' says his brother, 'I was never afraid of getting hurt. The only thing I was scared of was losing a tackle. Being defeated in a tackle.'

'Is that a bloke thing? A pride thing?'

'Probably. Tackling is the most cathartic part of the whole game. Much better than kicking goals.'

'Specially,' says Amby, 'when you hurt a guy but without actually injuring him. You hear him groan, but then he gets up and he's all right.'

—

I've read that old people need less sleep. I'm getting less, and I need more. I wake at 5 am weighed down by dull, old-person's hopelessness. I must have been mad to start this book. How can I wriggle out of it? And so on. My feet hurt when they meet the wooden floor. But I get up. I do the chooks. I cheat to finish the quick crossword. I open the footy pages and here it comes again to save me, the thrill of this crazy language they use. 'A surfeit of clean, crisp waves from half-back.' 'They butchered a prime opportunity to chew into the deficit early in the third stanza.' 'Anything that was shallow, they rebounded.' 'We missed sitters early, then they went bang, bang, bang.' 'I'm optimistic about the group's character but talk's cheap.' And I search up on YouTube and watch, again and again, Artie Jones's astonishing final-quarter goal against Carlton: running at top speed he snatches the ball with both hands from the air beside him, curves to his left and blasts it through. Why does this make me shout and cry? His jubilant teammates go bounding towards him. Jones throws himself into the arms of Rory Lobb who in a wild hug lifts him right off his feet with his legs dangling, like a father exulting in a son. Jamarra Ugle-Hagan, more formally, takes Jones's head in his two great hands, as one would to bless a child.

—

Two remarkable men, maybe in their forties, Cameron and Dean, on *7.30*. They and some other passing tradies were the first people to run to a bus that had been smashed and thrown on to its side in a collision with a truck: a bus full of trapped, injured, screaming primary-school children. Cameron is able to talk, to answer questions, but the other man, Dean—his face is blank and smooth with shock. It hurts to look at him. He can hardly speak: 'They were just...stuck, poor little things.' The men tore the skylight covers off the bus roof, they tried to *dig a hole* under the bus to free the kids—all their lunchboxes and jackets flung out and strewn across the bitumen—but they couldn't lift it. They 'held the children's hands and covered them with their jumpers to protect them from the cold'. The program's presenter, famous for her cool self-command, breaks free of it to praise these men who ran straight into the disaster. She wants to pay tribute to their guts and nerve. She leans forward over her desk and in a voice that trembles she thanks them, as if on behalf of their fellow citizens who are watching, faint with horror.

—

On Saturday afternoon we watch the Bulldogs beat the Adelaide Crows. An unattractive, even ugly game on a wet ground in Ballarat. Awful piles of scrambling, writhing men. 'We won,' says Amby's dad, 'but we didn't actually play well.'

And on Sunday the Colts play Hoppers Crossing, down at our oval. I'm so low-spirited, driving to the ground after hours on my knees weeding in the sodden backyard, that I'm starting to wonder if this is depression. It's cold, a south-westerly comes and goes. The elm leaves are only now starting to turn; with each flood of wind they release a shower of delicate yellow dots.

Amby's mum and dad have brought our dog Smokey on a lead, which they loop around a fence post. We stand at the rail in the north-east corner, the spot from which we observed the famous brawl—'the incident'—so earth-shattering at the time but now forgotten, never mentioned. The waters have closed over it. Silas is back from suspension. The season rolls on.

Archie's parents join us.

'See that boundary umpire?' says Archie's dad. 'That kid? Running in? He's a pro.'

'What?'

'He's getting paid. He gets fifty bucks a game.'

'He could do three in a weekend,' says Archie's mum. 'That's $150. And it's a pathway. Towards doing it as a job.'

This one looks no older than ten, thin and light-framed, and fiercely concentrating. When the ball goes over the line and he has to turn his back to the field for the throw-in, he adopts a formal posture, holding the ball in two hands, vertical, by its tips—a lovely moment of pause—then down he folds and hurls it back over his head with an effort so great that his spine arcs like a bow.

Smokey is let off the lead to play with his friend, the coach's family dog. They roll on the grass, growling, gnawing at each other's necks and cheeks. The play surges towards our goal and, bloody hell, Smokey's in there frolicking among the shouting, straining players, grinning like an idiot.

'Smokey! Smokey! Get over here!'

He hurries off the field, head down. 'He must have heard Amby's voice,' says Amby's flustered mum. And that voice is loud. He yells hoarsely, like a madman or a drunk.

The wind gets up, I am having to hold on to my hat.

'It doesn't look like it on the scoreboard,' says Archie at half-time, 'but we're dominating this game. We're a better team. We can win this.'

Three-quarter time: three points the difference and we're in front.

'Now the wind's against us,' says Archie.

I stand beside his mum at the southern boundary. Meth races past us with the ball, he kicks it way forward and a large, chunky Hoppers Crossing boy goes at him behind the play, shoves him in the chest, curses him out, swings his foot right up and hooks his ankle round Meth's neck. A blast of rage goes through me. I scream like some mouthy slag in the outer: 'Yew bloody thug!' There's no umpire in view! It will go unpunished! But Meth fights for balance, shoves him off and dashes away. Tag as they might, Hoppers Crossing can't stop this lithe boy, he's a streak of fire.

Later, after we've won, I ask Amby, 'Where was the umpire?'

He shrugs. 'They were hopeless. We were all yelling the kid's number but nobody did anything.'

In the rooms Archie's mum stands beside me near the door, listening to her son praising his team, her head lowered to hide her enormous smile.

Amby heaves his bike into the boot of the car. 'I didn't play well.'

'You did so! I saw you!'

'Yes but I kept dropping the ball. I gave away four free kicks.'

'Want to stop for some hot chips?'

'No. I want something fresh and crisp.'

My 'depression' is gone. Is this what Amby means when he talks about 'getting my anger out'? I'm old and sad and angry about the world, and I know it's too late for me to do anything to heal it—but maybe screaming counts?

—

Amby reports on the way to training that Silas is injured. 'He's not allowed to train all week and not allowed to play for seven days. But he says he's going to play on Sunday.'

'Is he trying to make up for the brawl?'

'No.'

'Are people still talking about it?'

'No. Some of the parents were upset about it but the coach and the players aren't talking about it any more.'

He lopes away. I position myself at the rail. By 6 pm it's totally dark. Angus arrives, morose, dangling his bag by its cord off one finger. He stands looking out over the field with its cold lights. Still in his reverie, before he runs out to join the kick to kick, he unclasps a fine chain from round his neck, runs it loose into one palm, and stoops to stow it in the pocket of his backpack.

I feel oddly distant from everything. No spark. Is it Covid still affecting me? In ten minutes I am chilled right through and starting to shake. Low blood sugar. I haven't brought money. For the first time since I started this watching, I walk away from it. I drive home, collect my card and a water bottle, and come back via Coles where I buy two small bottles of juice and five black sesame frozen mochis. (Why do they always come up half-price at checkout? Not that I'm complaining.) Back at the park I sit in the car in the dark, guzzling and reading texts on my phone. I don't think I'll come to training any more. It's winter. I'm too old. Or too something. Or no longer enough something. Some light in me is fading. Is almost extinguished.

At 7.20 I force myself out into the cold and watch the last ten minutes of the practice match against the U18s. 'JakeJake-Jake!' 'SeanySeanySeany!' *Whack*! *Thump*! Remy's mighty, howling voice: 'Here here here!' 'Behind, behind!' 'Again, again, again!'

My heart gives a big pump and I'm awake. I see Amby deliver a couple of tremendous soaring kicks and take a wild leaping-backwards mark out in the centre of the field.

When he gets into the car beside me (his great mannish bare thighs, the sharp smell of exertion) he heaves a deep, happy sigh. 'Well, that was the best footy I've ever played. Why can't I play like that in games? If I'd played like that on Sunday I'd've been best on ground.'

Was it because I wasn't watching that he trained so well? This is not about you, dopy nanna. He didn't even notice you weren't there.

—

On Thursday, for the first time except when I had Covid or was at the opera, I don't go to training at all. It's too cold, it's too dark, I don't feel like it. But even comfortable at home on the couch, absorbed in Prince Harry's memoir, I miss it. 'Our' team.

—

And 'we' beat Yarraville! In heavy rain and on a field so slippery they can hardly stay on their feet. Amby plays with grit and power. At three-quarter time his face, in the huddle, is dark with determination, manly, staring: I'm almost scared of him. Silas's grandmother and I, having learnt that we have the same first name, yell even more wildly. In the third quarter a

Yarraville player goes down hard in the goal square. He lies still, on his back. A terrible hush. The trainers run for a stretcher and six men carry him away. Both teams come off smeared with dark muck, like creatures from the Black Lagoon. From Amby's left knee runs a bent trickle of blood that only a nanna could perceive between the streaks of slime. In the rooms they sing and roar in their filth. An old man in a rain hood turns to me and says joyfully, 'What did you think of *that*?'

—

At training tonight I watch the way each of the boys, taking advantage of a free moment, will kick for goal on an impossible angle, trying to curve it, to score a banana. Before they go home the word comes: the Yarraville boy who went down yesterday is not injured, no, he is fine.

In the car Amby says to me, in a low voice, 'I concussed a kid once, in U10s.'

'Was he out cold?'

'No.' He mimics a stunned rolling, closing, half-opening of the eyes. 'It was awful.'

'Were there hard feelings?'

'No. Everyone knew it was an accident.'

—

I have a lawyer friend in Sydney who worked for several years at the Royal Commission into Institutional Child Abuse. The only way she could bear the work without cracking up, she says, was to go back to playing the piano, which she was once good at but had abandoned when she went into law. She bought a fat book of Mozart's keyboard music, and when she came home each evening, sickened and weary, she would sit down and work her way through a sonata. I tell her what I'm trying to write about.

'We've been approached,' she tells me, 'to support many men in Melbourne who were sexually abused as children within football clubs. We've had no luck engaging with the higher echelons of Victorian football. Do you want to learn more?'

No, no, no, no, no. I don't. What a fool I am, I think, stumping home from Pilates, to idealise the game, depicting it as a Homeric struggle full of noble manly customs and ethical training for teenage boys—and now I'm told that it's corrupted, shot through with evil, just like everything else in this world. Why the hell am I shocked? How could it be otherwise? It's a bloody institution, and this is Planet Earth.

Why don't I keep my mouth shut when people ask me what I'm writing? I'm surprised how many people jump to the conclusion that it's something polemical, a critical study of football culture and its place in society, informative, analytical, statistical. Really I'm trying to write about footy and my grandson and me. About boys at dusk. A little life-hymn. A poem. A record of a season we are spending together before he turns into a man and I die.

June

Amby is sick today, a sore throat. He lies on the couch next door. Halfway through the afternoon he texts me: 'Did you ever cook those parsnips we bought?'

—

A new player comes to the Bulldogs in a mid-season draft: a dark-haired twenty-year-old with a dramatically hollow-cheeked face, a long straggly mullet and a moustache. 'Poulter,' reports the *Age*, 'says his best attributes are probably his running capacity and ball use by foot. "My run-and-carry—I mostly play across wing and half-back, so I try to use my legs a lot. I feel like I've got something of a nice kick too, so just trying to penetrate and get…"' Here in my notebook there's a scrawl down the page where I fell asleep.

—

'I'm all for the beast and the rage,' writes my niece's partner, a professor of German. 'I know exactly the state of feeling at three-quarter time that you observe in these boys, though for me, in rugby league and soccer, there was only one break, at half-time, with the obligatory quartered oranges. I could measure the state of my own inner demon by my response to those orange segments. Later on I became interested in on-field ethics: what do you do when you catch yourself in the middle of an animal reaction, or when you suffer one from another? Many times I was told in the heat of battle that I would be carted away "in a body bag". Once I was walloped from behind at the end of a match we'd won easily by a hot-headed Argentine. He could have broken my jaw—I was lucky. I had put in three goals, and had responded to taunts that lasted beyond the end of the game with a final jibe: "What's the score, mate?" That's when the fist was swung.'

—

'Back in the U10s,' says Amby at the kitchen table, 'we were playing a really dirty team—they'd kick you and punch you and stuff. This day we were winning by two or three goals, and one of their kids finally kicked a goal, it was a really good goal, and running past he turned to me and gave me two fingers and said, "Cop that, cunt." I was like, "I've never heard someone say *that* before! That's so *rude*!" I told my dad about it in the car on the way home, and he said, "Ambrose, never call anyone a cunt," and I was like, "No, I won't I won't I won't!" But I did, in the match. Yesterday.'

'*Oowah*. Did anyone notice?'

'The kid I said it to noticed.'

'Was he offended?'

'I don't think so.'

—

Amby has Covid again. No training all week. But by Sunday morning, having tested negative for two days, he gets up and insists on playing. I have to go to a friend's eightieth birthday lunch, and miss seeing Newport beat us by two points. Amby's dad says the umpiring was 'outrageous: four dubious frees in the last quarter'.

On Monday morning Amby comes into my kitchen at 7.30.

'I need three oranges.'

He's wearing a white singlet and his hair is wet from the shower. He puts a big arm round me: 'Did I tell you I was second-best on ground?'

'Hurray!'

He allows himself to beam and laugh.

'And who was first?'

In chorus we say, 'Jake.'

Jake is their top player. He always gets best on ground.

—

Two guys are here cleaning my windows.

I say to the young one, 'Do you play footy?'

'No. But I like it.'

'Do you follow a team?'

'Yep. Collingwood.'

'Oooh. You must be happy this season.'

'Yeah.'

'I follow the Western Bulldogs.'

'They're a good team.'

'Yeah but they fall apart in the third quarter and I don't know why.'

He shrugs, wringing out a rag: 'That's footy.'

—

Monday evening and now Archie's got Covid. The boys are going to run their own training tonight, without him. This I have got to see.

Archie's dad turns up at the rail with a message. 'Lachie Neale of Brisbane,' he tells me in his genial way, 'says he makes sure he touches the ball at least a thousand times every day and that's why he never fumbles. So Archie wants me to tell the team they have to touch it three hundred times.'

I'm not sure if I'm supposed to laugh but I can't help it.

He laughs too: 'When he was a kid Archie loved organising the others to play competitive games—we always used to hear him barking out the scores.'

He moves on, with his dog. I am now the only adult present.

Not that anyone notices or cares. As always I am invisible to them. It's dark, the tall lights are blazing down; lucky I wore my hat. I lean on the rail close to where the boys dump their bags and jackets and street shoes and water bottles. They greet each other with a quick palm tap, the arm low and loosely slung. Here comes Boof, back from injury. Everyone loves Boof. When he's away something is lacking. He radiates good cheer and confidence: his sweet, handsome face, his muscly legs, his solid, unshowy skills. While he is emptying stuff out of his backpack, talking and laughing, he takes two big sucks on an asthma puffer.

In charge seems to be Remy, the biggest and most manly looking of them all, a natural leader, with the loudest and most carrying voice. Without their coach the boys are milling about near the goal square, at a loss, idly kicking the yellow balls at the posts and into the darkness over near the skate ramp.

Remy rounds them up, calls them to order: 'Boys—no muckin' round, right? Don't kick—don't *kick. Boys.* If you kick, go get the ball—I saw you kick that!'

They start the first complex manoeuvre, running and handball, shouting each other's names in triplets. The intimacy, the binding force of a name, always drawing the team together, knowing each other, calling on each other: *Trust me! I'm here! I'm ready!*

A father comes to the rail a few metres along from me; have I met him? I stay where I am for a while, then edge towards him. He greets me with a nod and a smile.

'Hi,' I say. 'Which one's yours?'

'Anthony.'

'Anthony?'

'Boof.'

'Oh! I'm Amby's grandmother.'

'I knew Amby in the Under-10s.'

While we watch he yarns to me about the days when he coached them: 'They were so little then. Look at 'em now! They're nearly men!'

'Why is Boof called Boof?'

He pulls out his phone: a little boy with a mass of black curls bursting out around his head.

'He always had this *huge* hair. And look at this.'

The next photo shows a boy's head in profile, buzz-cut to the scalp, and beside it, on a table, a great mass of thickly plaited dark hair.

'It was for charity. They raised $7000 from it. They donated the money to the Children's Hospital, and the hair went to a charity that makes wigs for kids who've lost their hair because of their medical conditions.' He puts the phone in his pocket. 'You couldn't say Boof was a natural footballer. He used to be chubby. He loved everything about footy except running. But he's always had an old head on his shoulders. He knew he wasn't going to get anywhere. So he put his mind to it. He busted his bum. At his first three training sessions he threw up.'

On the field someone is down. Others pause and glance back at him.

I make a nanna sound: 'Oooh, I hate to see them drop.'

The boy struggles to his feet and plods on.

'Yeah, injuries,' says Boof's dad. 'It's a rough game.'

'Do you get scared?'

He looks at me: 'Scared?'

'There's no point getting scared, is there,' I say hastily.

A pause.

'I've noticed,' he says, turning back to the play, 'that it's the ones who go half…the ones who are a bit…timid, a bit slow, who hold back—they're the ones who get hurt. The little ones, the ones who are very quick, they can get themselves out of trouble. But I remember Amby, from the first time I knew him, he never held back. He's always gone in hard.'

Three other fathers who have joined us at the rail are amazed at how well-organised and hard-working the boys are tonight, without their coach.

'They're really turning themselves into a team now, aren't they,' I say.

'Yep,' says Tommy and Ned's dad. 'A couple of years ago without a coach they would've just come down into the goal square and kicked bananas for an hour.'

—

A bye this Sunday so quite a few boys are missing from Thursday training. A beautiful night, dark but clear. In sharp winter air the big city buildings on the eastern skyline are no more than a thousand tiny squares of gold on a wall of black velvet. Meth is sick with a bad cold. But Archie is back from

Covid: 'I slept for forty-eight hours and then I was fine. Come on, boys! Spread it out! Twenty-metre kicks!'

Their splintering howls. The constant hand-tapping, the tiny salutes. 'Get dangerous!' 'I *am* dangerous!' I will never cease to wonder at the way a kicked ball will bounce energetically towards the boundary, and turn back on itself and stop just before it crosses the line.

'I'm gonna pick six of you,' shouts Archie, 'and ask you to tell me a good thing and a bad thing about what we were doing in that drill!'

Their replies are out of earshot. In a ring they gather, all except Angus, who loiters behind the circle on his own, stooping to examine his shin, stroking it, then standing with his arms folded and one leg extravagantly bent, gazing at the ground. Tonight he is irritable, harassing people, pushing at anyone who comes near him. He hooks his leg round another boy's ankle, grabs his thigh with both hands and yanks at it. They are getting cranky with him. One kid seems to be holding another one back from rushing at him.

The wind changes and the temperature drops. I'm shivering on the back of my bench, against which a boy of eight or so, someone's patient younger brother, has parked his pushbike. I huddle in my thin coat and watch how this kid, the minute the team stampedes away to the other end of the ground, takes his chance to launch a furtive kick for goal with one of the spare balls that are scattered about on the grass. He misses. Tries again. Sees me watching and tries harder. Scores. Walks away with exaggerated casualness. Notices that his bike is leaning against my bench and runs to move it: 'Sorry!'

On the drive home, Amby, panting and sweating beside me, says, 'Well, I'm back.'

'Back? Your injuries are gone?'

'Yep. My leg. It's stopped hurting. I trained really well.'

A sense of calm fills the car, a pleasant element in which we bask as we fly down the hill past the Women's Peace Garden and up to the intersection near the racecourse.

I say, 'What was bugging Angus tonight?'

'I dunno. He kept complaining that no one was kicking to him. So when I took a mark I kicked it straight to him, a really good kick, and he dropped it. So after that nobody kicked it to him.'

—

On the 59 tram a young black man holds tenderly on his lap a four-level, rubber-band-strapped, open-sided container. Of eggs. A man carrying a hundred and twenty eggs? He sees me clock them, and flashes me a 100-watt smile, a witty smile, an awareness of the strange figure he must cut.

—

Amby has resolved to concentrate on his schoolwork. There are more SACS coming up. I put my head round his door: the made bed, the cleared floor, the bare desk with the team photos stuck to the wall above.

'Good on you. That looks business-like.'

Against a wall, two surfboards lean in their bags.

'Why don't you put the boards in the shed?'

'Nah. I like to have them near me.'

—

Amby's mum and I have a coffee and a toastie in a bar on Little Bourke Street. Music is playing through a very classy system. While we eat we observe, through the tall windows, a man lying on a crude pile of bedding in the doorway of a shut-down business on the other side of the narrow street. He's fifty or so, balding, tall, hard-faced from street living, but occupying his possie with ease. He lies back talking and laughing and listening, in the company of his imaginary friends. I keep glancing over at him: his mouth opens and shuts, as if in genial speech; he closes it while his phantom companions make their contributions; he smiles and laughs and adds a comment, then relaxes for a while, on his back, letting his gaze roam over the stained and peeling wall of his temporary accommodation. He is a man in command of his situation. It's impossible to imagine any authority figure with the nerve, what my mother used to call 'the hide', to order him to move on.

—

On Friday night Amby and his mate Macca go to Marvel to see the Bulldogs v Port Adelaide. I watch it on TV, a shocking nailbiter. Port Adelaide are a terrific team but to me hateable—a tendency to a sort of grinning violence. In a melee, a Dogs player lands on his back on the ground, a Port guy presses him down, and grabs his balls! He gropes for them! It's unmistakeable! Blow the whistle! A couple of nasty little fights, and the Dogs *cannot* kick goals—this is getting to be psychological. And yet after the siren my nerves are soothed by the way the two teams mingle—guys talking and shaking hands and laughing after two hours at each other's throats.

Macca sleeps over at my place. Late in the morning I hear men's voices talking somewhere in the house. I stick my head around the door of the spare room. It's Amby and Macca hard at work, analysing the game while they remake the bed Macca slept in.

'How about last night!' I say.

'Oh,' says Macca, 'it was terrible. Shocking. And the umpiring! The umpiring was *insane*. When they reversed that goal! They *reversed* it! That was so *destructive*!'

Amby says nothing, concentrating hard on the piece of housework. They are making a meal of it—turning the doona this way and that, edging round the bed with armfuls of cushions and pillows, rearranging, resquaring, examining the result with heads on one side, attacking again, always with deep seriousness and a complete lack of understanding of the simplicity of the job. Now they are going out skating.

While I wash up I put on my new headphones and listen to three footy commentators talking about the Western Bulldogs, whose coach, Luke Beveridge, seems to be losing his grip: the

Dogs are a team packed with first-rate players but, for reasons no one understands, Beveridge keeps moving certain men to different positions each week, causing the team to collapse and get thrashed.

Commentator 1: (solemnly) 'Bevo's like a bloke who's got a magnificent sports car but he's putting the wrong fuel in it.'

Commentator 2: (with a flippant laugh) 'Where'd you get *that* from?'

Commentator 1: (loftily) 'It's a *metaphor*, mate.'

Commentator 3: (excitedly) 'Yeah! He's got a Ferrari and he's puttin' diesel in it!'

I while away the rest of the morning on YouTube, where I stumble on 'The Greatest AFL Torps of All Time'. My God, those tiny shorts they wore in the 80s! Astonishingly enormous, sky-scraping kicks. It doesn't matter how often the torp is explained to me, I still could not define it to save my life. And yet I get absolute goose bumps at the crazed, cracked-voiced yelling of the commentator: 'And 'e's gorn the *TOOOOOORP!*'

———

In the kitchen Amby tosses the coffee grounds into the compost bucket. I always need to scrape them in, but he does it with one sharp tap and a flick of the wrist.

'Do you notice that as you get stronger, from footy, your… abilities have increased? I mean, in normal daily life?'

'Yep. It's easier to do things. Loosen things.'

—

On the Western Bulldogs website I watch Bob Murphy, their beloved former captain, being inducted into the team's Hall of Fame. Something undefended in his face, his quiet decency, always moves me. His curly brown hair is going grey. From the pocket of his suit he draws a screwed-up sheet of punched paper and glances at what he's scribbled on it. 'There's a lot of emotive language these days around "family". But footy's not *The Brady Bunch*. It's a hard game. It *exposes* you. It exposes all your shortcomings, as well as your talents. I jarred my finger one time, in a training session. I'm going, "I jarred m' finger." And Tony Liberatore snarls at me, "Ya got nine more."'

The revved-up interviewer asks him if his kids and grand-kids will be proud of him for this honour.

'My children,' says Murphy drily, 'have a healthy disregard for my football career.'

—

I come to at 3 am in a weird blurred panic, cold legs, cold feet, still in the world of a dream but thinking I'm awake: I've forgotten to write something about a different sort of footy, not AFL, that I've become aware of and am studying. The ball has a strange shape and a hard, metallic sparkle, the players are dressed in loose white garments. I swim out of this very slowly, in terrific anxiety. How can I have neglected this duty? Where are my notes? What have I done with my *notes?* Without my notes I won't be able to remember any of the games! The details, the events will have escaped me. I'm weak with fear and despair. But as I lie there, sick about it, and my mind focuses itself and returns to me bit by bit, I hear myself say out loud, 'It was a *dream* football!' I rearrange my bedclothes and go back to sleep.

—

I pull a muscle in my back when making a tiny arm movement to take a scarf out of the cupboard. My Pilates teacher works on my soreness. It hurts more and more, spreads right across the small of my back; bit by bit it subsides, and by evening it's gone.

—

I drive Amby to training and leave him there. To make up for this dereliction I go to the Bulldogs website and study the players at training, their graceful bodies, and Brad Johnson (in our family always referred to as 'Bran Johnsa', as Amby when small thought he was called) rattling on in his merry way about the team's chances this weekend against North Melbourne. I watch a bit of Port Adelaide v Geelong. First time in my life I shout for the Cats.

—

When I pick Amby up at the park they are playing the U18s. I watch vaguely for the last ten minutes. Down near the eastern goal there's a brief commotion: somebody's made a mistake, kids yell, and one of the U18s, a short, bristly-headed, chunky, dangerous-looking guy who a moment earlier has kicked for goal, a set shot, and missed, bellows, 'What are ya doing, ya bloody idiot? Go home! Go home! GO HOME!'

—

Amby thinks he might have broken his pinkie. I forbear to say, 'Ya got nine more.' He shows me his palm. A faint but unmistakeable purple stain is spreading from the swollen area near his little finger. He doesn't complain. In fact he seems proud of it.

'Maybe it's not broken?' I say. 'Maybe it's just really badly bruised?'

'Maybe,' he says calmly. 'I'll strap it.'

Is this what they call 'carrying an injury through a season'?

—

On Sunday we verse Williamstown. Bayside College has three immense ovals, all of them lacking in any form of seating or fences or even rails to lean on. Just this vast, mown field, covered in lakes of rain from the night before. Whenever someone goes down in a tackle, bright sheets of water fly up. We can't help laughing, it's so extreme and ridiculous.

Cold wind, cold sun.

'It's a crystal-clear day,' says Amby's dad. 'The gumtrees are swaying. How's the lean on that goalpost! Maybe they'll swap them over with each quarter.'

The siren is weirdly shrill and feeble. On this huge ground I strain to follow. Everything is so far away. Five or six times in the match the action veers close to our bunch of parents, where I'm standing beside Meth's mum—the thick of it is almost in our faces. We rear back from its speed, the shoving, grunting bodies, the hoarse shouting: 'Handball! You're hot! Handball!' The coloured boots thundering, the mud, the mad concentration of the faces. Where are our boys? There's Meth, breaking away from the pack, we're all screaming his name, 'Meth! Meth! Go Meth!'

And for the first time I am invited to be one of the ladies who take out the oranges at the break.

'Go on, Hel!' says Amby's mum, who is the one actually rostered on. '*You* do it!'

I gasp. 'Me? How do you do it?'

'How do you think? Soon as the siren goes, you walk out to the huddle, take the lid off the box and hold it out to them!'

To the huddle? By myself? In the corner of my eye the delicate fur trim of Meth's mum's raincoat hood quivers in the wind.

'Come with me?'

Out we go, picking our way across the soaked and trampled grass. We are very small and shy and thrilled, holding out our offering, the big square plastic box of orange wedges and a brown paper bag for the skins. The mud-streaked, panting boys jostle around us, tower over us, grabbing the fruit in their fists and to my amazement politely saying thank you! Smiling at us! Up close, oh, their soft faces and special haircuts, their pimples, their nascent moustaches. We love them. It's an honour and a joy to serve them.

Late in the final quarter, when we're well ahead, a brawl breaks out way over on the other side of the ground.

Archie mutters to himself, 'Oh, why do we have to *do* this?'

Here comes Angus, trudging all the way back to the coach's box.

Trainer: (indignant) 'Joo get sennoff?'

Angus: (in low voice) 'Apparently I started it.'

Archie: 'What happened?'

Angus: 'Apparently I hit him.'

Archie: 'Now we're one man down. There's got to be something in this.' (To the runner). 'Go and tell the umpire we've only got seventeen men.'

Runner returns: 'He says we can send one on but not Angus.'

Archie: 'They're scared of you, Angus.'

I think he must get what they call 'the red mist'. And he's suspended for a week. Just before the final siren Liam, who has come off, stands on the boundary next to his coach, huge shudders running down him from head to foot.

—

The Bulldogs beat North Melbourne. That Bont. His quiet, faithful brilliance. Where does such a man come from? Cody Weightman kicks six goals and executes a magnificent screamer: he romps up the back of North's Griffin Logue in great strides, like a man bounding up a staircase. Later I roam around the internet feasting on Weightman in the air, the commentator howling for him as he flies above six-foot-ten Max Gawn: '*Weightmaaaaaaaan!* What about that climb! Tiny little man just sat on Max's head!'

—

Amby seems in rather low spirits.

'Is it your "broken" finger that's bothering you?'

'No. It aches a bit but I strap it for training and matches.'

'You don't seem happy. What's up?'

'Girls,' he says, 'are the bane of my existence.'

I decide not to ask for particulars. In the kitchen his dad is turning out delicious little pizzas with garlic, anchovies and thin slices of mozzarella. We get into a conversation about Catholic guilt.

'I don't know,' I say, 'why Catholics always talk about guilt as if they had it worse than Protestants. You're allowed to confess and be forgiven. We have to carry it on our own. There's no priest between us and God.'

Amby's dad, a disgusted ex-Catholic, several of whose teachers are now in jail for sexual abuse, tells about the ridiculous little sins he used to invent for weekly confession in boarding school. He has nothing but impatience and scorn for the sacrament.

'Did you ever confess sincerely?'

'NO!'

'Why didn't you?'

'Because I didn't BELIEVE in it! I was a thirteen-year-old boy! I hadn't DONE anything!'

His two sons stand leaning against the kitchen bench, chewing the salty morsels, listening, saying nothing.

—

Turns out Angus has been suspended for two weeks because of the brawl, and so has the boy from Williamstown. Someone told Amby that our club has been fined $500, but Amby doesn't know if it's true. We talk about the red mist. Amby's mum asks him if he has experienced it. He says no.

'When a fight starts are you tempted to get into it?'

He says he is, but that he's always been too far away. His dad tells the story of a fight he and his friends John and Hernie got into one night in a pizza shop on Chapel Street, back in the 80s. Two nasty guys drive up in a red Porsche and barge in trying to pick a fight, despite the presence of several families with young kids quietly eating at the tables. One of the guys grabs Hernie by his ponytail and drags his head to the floor, yelling, 'Why don't you get a fuckin' job, you wanker?'

'Hernie,' says Amby's dad, his cheeks flushing even now with rage, 'was a fitter and turner. He was the most...

hard-working...so I'—he pauses, looks at us two women with an awkward smile—'I don't know how to tell this story. Should I make out I was the hero who saved his friend, or—'

'Maybe just tell the facts? And don't interpret them?'

'Okay. I grabbed the guy who'd attacked Hernie and I got him up against their red car and I punched him in the face. I hit him and hit him and hit him.'

'Did you knock him out?' says Amby's mum.

'I don't think so. But it was a long time ago. Next day my hand was infected. Because human teeth are full of bacteria. Next door to where I worked there was a vet. He gave me some antibiotics. He said, "Don't worry—they're exactly the same as the ones humans take."'

'Did the two guys drive away in their Porsche?'

'No. They kept chasing us. We were in our band van. We didn't know who they were or who they knew or who their friends were—they might've known bikies—so we drove to the St Kilda police station and parked outside, and stayed there till they drove away.'

We all sit in silence, thinking. The boys' faces are sobered. Is it possible for them to imagine their dad doing these things? *Having* to do them?

—

Winter solstice and no one's watching training but me.

'The first ball to hit the ground,' shouts Archie, 'five push-ups.'

It's cold enough for gloves. Angus strips off his jumper and trains in nothing but baggy shorts and a white singlet. Whenever he can slide away he is to be seen on his own kicking for goal. It starts to rain, light but steady. My straw hat is getting wet. I hold out for fifteen minutes and crack. I trot back to my car, where I have nothing to entertain me. The windows fog up. I can hear a distant voice shouting: it's Archie, giving orders. I try to do some thinking, to pass the remaining hour in a useful way. At last Amby gets in, sopping, with dripping hair. As we pull out from the kerb I spot a tall gangly boy being dinked away into the dark on the bar of a smaller kid's pushbike: he's hunched over, his head screwed to one side, grinning and waving.

'My God,' I say. 'It's Angus. Being dinked.'

'He can just be so...*annoying*. He used to be a bit of a ratbag, years ago. One time in a contest we were running for the ball, I got to it first, I picked it up. It was still cricket season, we couldn't wear boots on the pitch. I did like a sharp turn, the grass was wet and slippery, he tried to chase me but he slid and fell over. He got up and yelled for Archie with his arms out. He said, "Why can't we have boots yet?" And I said, "Even if you had boots you couldn't catch me." Then right through that season at training, just us two would start pushing and shoving and getting in each other's face—*You're shit! You're shit!* Nobody said it but there was a mutual understanding that we both really wanted to try hard. And we'd go hard together. I really, really like him now.'

—

I boast to my Newcastle friend about having been one of the orange ladies. I describe Meth's mum and me timidly approaching the players, holding out the box of fruit and the paper bag. He can't stop laughing: 'It's like Bullen's African Lion Safari!'

—

Now I've caught a revolting cold. Nosebleeds, streaming snot, razorblade throat, feeble scraping cough. Covid negative, but for days not a soul comes near me or remembers I exist. I lie dismally in bed with my hot water bottle, half stunned, full of self-pity, listening to Radiohead on YouTube. How can I never have heard them before? I miss Amby's match against Werribee Centrals. I have to send texts pleading for news.

My sister: 'We're ahead 3/4 time. 39:16. There was a "spy"! Near the coach's box! They said they heard Archie call one of their players a wanker! They're threatening to report him! It's worse than the Stasi!'

Nobody comes in to announce the Colts' triumph. Here I lie, forgotten, wallowing in my bitterness.

At last Amby texts: 'Spewing you weren't there. I took a huge mark against their ruck. Here's a photo. I am terribly sore. Every time I jumped in the ruck the other guy kneed me. My hips and chest are sore.'

'He kneed you? Give me his address. (Hammer, bomb

and coffin emojis).'

'I still smoked him though.'

'Dat's my boy. Was your crush there?'

'No she was not. She had work.'

'Aw. This won't be your last huge mark.'

'I hope not.'

I forward the photo of the mark to my Newcastle friend. He replies, 'They look like twisting supplicants in a Blake print.' I can always rely on him to see the poetry in things.

———

Archie swears black and blue that he did *not* call one of the Werribee Centrals players a wanker.

'We were winning by about fifty points—there'd be no reason for me to engage in verbal warfare with a fourteen-year-old.' But the other coach was so mad at him after the game that he wouldn't shake hands; he just walked away. Archie was surprised, and dismayed. 'I was like, aw shit! That was pretty full-on!'

———

A plumber turns up at 7 am to mend a hole in my roof: a six-foot, black-bearded young tradie in a dark-blue boilersuit, with shining eyes and a warm smile. As he's propping his ladder, our dog Smokey starts barking in the kitchen.

'I love dogs,' he says. 'I had two but they died.'

'Ohhh. God bless them. It's the saddest thing, when a dog dies.'

He stands still. A wave of something passes over his face. His eyes glisten.

'I've got their names on my neck,' he says, drawing aside his collar: under his ear a large tattoo of intricately runic lettering.

Dead dogs are my link with this sweetly emotional stranger. I could tell him about Dozer, who's buried under the crepe myrtle just behind where he's standing, but it's his sorrow we're talking about, not mine.

———

Amby and his dad have gone surfing. Footy's no fun when they're out of town. Swans v Cats. What is it with these goddamn moustaches? They should be against the law. They make a man look vain, and shallow. A game between two teams I don't care about. Why bother?

But a couple of small human things will always happen. A Swans player who looks like one of the BeeGees gets a set shot right in front of goal. He can't miss, but he does. Cut to the box where Buddy Franklin and some other famous guy are watching. They turn to each other with their mouths sagging open. 'The unmissable,' announces the commentator, 'has been missed.' And at the end, after the Swans have kicked miserably and it's a draw, and while Geelong fans are hanging over the fence waving signs begging the players to give them their *boots*, for God's sake—when did THAT become a thing?—the Swans player who kicked three behinds in a row slinks off the ground in shame, eyes down. But one of his teammates puts out his arms, hugs him, and kisses him on the cheek. A kiss. A commiseration. All is not lost.

—

I ask Amby's dad about the rule for who jumps in a ball-up or a boundary throw-in. Do I hear the umpire call out their names?

'This,' he says, 'is one of those *stupidly* and *unnecessarily* complex rules the AFL comes up with. The rule is, one player from each team has to nominate himself to jump. Only one. It was originally to stop anybody else from rushing in.'

'Okay, but is it planned in advance? Before the match?'

'No. It's only for that particular moment.'

'I don't get it. What if more than one player nominates?'

'The first one to nominate gets it.'

'But what if two nominate at the same moment? Does the umpire decide?'

'The ruckman is usually there,' he says patiently, 'and that's who nominates.'

'And if he's not there, anyone can?'

'Yes.'

Long pause.

'And the umpire says the names of the two players who've nominated?'

'Yes. They usually know the names of every player on the

field. And if they don't, they go by numbers.'

But—how can they see the numbers without making them turn around? Pause, while I eat the pasta he's just served.

'It's bloody ridiculous,' he says. 'They come up with all these complex solutions to things that are hardly even problems. What *I* think they should do is, one man from each side goes up; and if a second player from one side goes up, the other side gets a free.'

I will never understand this game. Also, I don't care. I walk around the house thinking ignorantly about it, shouting, singing, talking to myself. All the time. Does this mean something about me? Something psycho, or scary?

July

I approach our park on a Sunday afternoon in July to watch Amby's team play Werribee District. A more junior match is in progress. The board shows a shocking score: HOME 00.00 (00) VISITORS 26.19 (175). Surely such numbers cannot be? Is it a joke? The siren sounds, the teams leave the ground. I don't think I should even look at them. I loiter under the trees near the cricket nets till the U16s come clattering out. How pale and dry-skinned and spotty the boys look in the cold winter sun.

They pause at the boundary gate. People on the field are holding up a banner for them to run through: 'REMY 100'. One hundred *games*? Or goals? Remy stands at the head of the line looking out at this tribute. His face is carefully composed. He launches himself towards the banner and the others surge behind him, cheering and clapping. I'm cheering too with a lump in my throat. He bursts through the banner tearing it into bright tatters.

I set out around the boundary, looking for someone to stand with. No one I know is here. At the timekeeper's table there's a man and a small woman, heads down studying a printed form. I don't know them. I keep walking, lonely and out of place: it's been school holidays, no training, I haven't been to the park for must be a fortnight, I've lost the feel of it.

I find a spot close to the box where the coach and trainers and runners stand. Silas's grandmother greets me. I'm glad to see her; we join forces, elbows on the rail.

Way over on the far side of the ground the team is gathered in a tight ring. They are roaring, and trampling their feet in a fast rhythm. Now, the solemn ritual of the bounce: the silence, the tense postures of readiness, the umpire's arms straightened above his head to present the ball, the powerful downward thrust, the explosion of movement. And the big men fly.

Archie's shouting: 'Hold your space! Go wide! Man on man! Know what, Ned? You can play wing. Go wherever you want. Stay wide.'

Angus, suspended for two weeks for the brawl, is here today in civvies, hanging out near the coach's box, wearing his pants fashionably halfway down his arse. Quarter time and the cold light flares in the hair of the team's two redheads. Boof kicks a goal. A big shout; they love him. Ned's head barely reaches Remy's shoulder yet he's vital, quicksilver, a strong kick. The water runner gives his job to Angus who is suddenly blessed with office. He stands beside Archie, who seems to be trying to hearten him, to make him feel valuable. Archie keeps calling to the players, always naming, naming: 'Good boy, Sam; good

one, Josh. One of you needs to lay a big tackle! Remy and
Jake! Come in! Get busy, boys!' The pack veers towards us
and explodes at our feet—we rear back—the sick thump of
bodies, their harsh open-mouthed breathing. Amby's in there
working, he slides past me, low to the ground, his face dark
as a fist.

Another goal and the loud slapping of palms. A rain shower
so fine and fragile I can see its slanting drops but can't feel
them. The winter sun is low and golden; the wind is sharp.

Third quarter. I move around closer to the goal, near a gap
in the fence. Suddenly they're thundering down on me, they're
going to trample me, I'm frozen, they won't stop, they can't
stop. I leap out of the way and the ball goes tumbling past
me over the boundary and under the fence towards the path
behind me. I turn and run after it, grab it off the ground with
both hands. God, I can't kick. What a fool I'd look. I raise it
above my shoulders and chuck it to the chubby little boundary
umpire who catches it and flashes me such a comradely smile
that for one second my whole existence is justified.

—

Amby and I are ready to drive to training. He comes out of
his bedroom singing and says to me, 'Do you want to fall in
love again?'

'No.'

'Why?'

'Because of the pain. Why do you ask?'

'I just heard a song that said, *I wanna fall in love again.*'

At that moment his older brother surges past us down the hall. I call after him teasingly, 'Are *you* in love?'

Instead of ignoring us he gives a blunt answer without breaking stride: 'Yes,' and vanishes into his room.

I turn around. Amby behind me, pulling his hoodie on, is staring at me with round eyes. We bare our teeth and raise our shoulders to our ears.

Later, after training, I pick him up, in the dark.

'How'd you go?'

'Good. Yeah. I played well. I know I always complain about having to go to training on Monday, because I'm always so sore from the game on Sunday. But if I've played badly on Sunday, like I did yesterday, training on Monday gives me a chance to redeem myself. And if I train well on Monday I'm good for the rest of the week.'

'You mean for footy?'

'For everything. School, footy, everything.'

———

Archie and I sit down at my kitchen table with a pot of tea and a couple of pastries. He's lanky and fine-boned (asthma from early childhood, then ballet, then hip hop), the sort of guy who has trouble sitting still. He tips this way and that on his chair, and throws himself back with his arms around his head when he laughs. I'm calling it an interview, but basically what we do is gossip and tell stories and psychologise impertinently about people's characters.

He's very happy with the way the season is going. 'The boys tell me the team's got the best chemistry it's ever had.'

Some of the things he says alarm me. 'You have to take risks, for the team to be good. You have to hurt yourself for it to be good. It's funny that we get so worried about unsportsmanlike acts, when really the whole game is unsportsmanlike. The reality is that you're playing a sport that you're going to get hurt in. And you know it. You walk out there every week knowing there's a chance you're going to get pretty badly injured. But everyone does it, and everyone loves it.'

We agree, though, that the game is a world in which a certain level of violence can be dealt with by means of ritual behaviour. I describe my favourite example of this: when, in 2022, Western Bulldogs' Bailey Smith headbutts Geelong's Zach Tuohy during an on-field brawl. The horror I feel at the snake-like lashing-out of Smith's head, his lightning-fast blow to Tuohy's forehead, the way Tuohy goes limp and stumbles back holding his head in both hands, the big red mark that springs out on his brow, his ripped jumper falling off his shoulder in rags. I have never before witnessed a headbutt. It makes me sick to my stomach. Smith is reported. After the final siren the two teams mingle on the ground. The camera picks up Tuohy, alone in the shot, walking with his right hand outstretched in a gesture that takes my breath away—is he—can he be—? The shot widens to include the man he's approaching: it's Smith, who turns to him and puts out his hand. They shake, they embrace, they walk away together with their arms across each other's shoulders, laughing.

Archie too laughs, in delight, at my astonishment and awe. 'That's *men*!' he cries.

And that's when he gives me the bad news: Boof is leaving town. He's about to go to the Northern Territory for a couple of months, on a long-planned school exchange. He'll miss the finals.

'Oh *no*. What will they do without him?'

'He's devastated. But he said, "If we make the grand final, Arch, I'll be back. I promise I'll be back."'

—

Dogs are versing Swans on Thursday night and Bailey Smith's not playing. I'm upset, but when I mention it to Amby he says he's *not* upset. He says he cares about the Bulldogs as a team but not so much about individual players.

'And anyway,' he says, arranging his long bare legs in the passenger footwell of the Corolla, 'often they say a player's sick when really he's been dropped.'

They do? This makes me feel even worse. I couldn't stand it if Smith, this shining, fast-moving star, should flare up and burn out. It's cold at training, already night. A sharp wind gets up. I've only worn a thin jacket. The boys are working with a will, but I'm shivering. I get back into the car and sit there brooding. I sneak home, pretending to myself it's to pick up a jumper, and turn on the TV at the very second when the umpire stretches both arms above his head to hail whatever deity watches darkly from among the stars. I stay on my feet, ready to hurry back to the park, but first I spar with Amby's dad in an enjoyable shouting match about Rory Lobb, who has also been dropped. I am disappointed for him, but my son-in-law is jubilant: he took against Lobb right back at the start of the season, whereas I have a soft spot for him because he reminds me of a long-ago boyfriend, a rangy great bunch of bones with a dramatic head and a rare, sweet smile.

I hang around, leaning over the couch back, for ten minutes, during which time the Bulldogs acquit themselves quite stylishly. Gee I love Cody Weightman! He always looks as if he's at a party—throwing himself with abandon into whatever's going on. He sails horizontally into tackles, rolls in a perfect somersault and bounds back to his feet. He's a muscly little sprite, hovering on the edge of laughter, bursting with goodwill, dancing in triumph, loving his teammates for their skill. I remember an old commentator beaming at the laughing, sweating, blissed-out boy after his debut with the Dogs: 'Thank you! For the joy you gave us!'

I tear back to the park and collect the filthy boy. We rush home to watch the Swans demolish us by two points. Oh, the cries and groans, the curses. And Buddy Franklin—shouldn't he have retired at the end of the '22 season, after millions of fans swarmed on to the ground to praise his thousandth goal? He's tired now, he's slowing down, his kicks go crooked; but I'll always love him for his dancer's walk, the way he puts the ball of his foot down first, like one of Milton's mighty angels, landing as if he weighed barely an ounce.

—

Where on earth is Manor Lakes? That's who we're playing this Sunday. At training one of the boys says it takes an hour to drive there. My hip sister, Amby's great-aunt, comes with us. Amby navigates. We get there in forty minutes.

The team warms up. Angus is playing kick to kick in socks and cheap thongs, waiting to be told to put his boots on.

'How light their touch is,' says my sister, 'when they mark!'

A young girl walks by with a bulldog on a leash. She pretends not to see us, lets it butt our legs aside as it passes. Three bigger girls stroll with feigned nonchalance along the boundary. Their thickly made-up leader snarls over her shoulder at her downcast acolytes, 'I had to walk round the *whole ground* to find you. And now I've got *rocks* in m' socks. For *no reason.*'

Joey's dad greets me outside the rooms. Rap, hip hop, whatever, is shaking the walls.

'Will they turn the music off when they start?'

'Oh,' he says, 'it's just the players getting themselves into the mood. I used to do that when I was a waiter. You wake up not feeling like it. I used to listen to Jimi Hendrix while I ironed my shirt.'

My brother turns up on his way home to the bush. 'Whenever my boys versed Mordi-Bayside, twenty years ago, there always used to be an ambulance in attendance. Even for the U16s.'

Silas's dad shows us a big yellow tube of a product he's

found called Griptek. 'You coat your palms with it so you can grip the ball when it's wet. Here, try it, Helen. Put some on.'

'No way! I've got to hold my notebook.'

He laughs, dropping it back in his camera bag. 'I put some on at the lights. And when they changed I couldn't unstick from the steering wheel.'

Here comes Meth, in street clothes. 'Hurt my shoulder at training. I'm taking a quick break.' Today he will run water.

Archie comes striding up in his baggy clothes. The teams run out. The umpires in yellow march on in procession. The siren. The bounce.

'Man up, Flemington!' shouts Archie. 'Spread, boys! Spread!'

The game hasn't been going long when I notice the Manor Lakes manager (a woman, like ours) heading purposefully along the boundary to the open-sided shelter where Archie is standing with the assistant coach, a trainer and a runner, a neat row of men at the very edge of the marked field. She's pointing with authority at their feet, gesturing sternly: apparently there's another, fainter line on the grass that they are failing to observe. With one accord, obeying her, the four men shuffle half a step backwards. Archie turns to watch her march back to her own team's shelter shed. His face is quite still, bright with incredulous surprise and suppressed laughter.

One of the Manor Lakes runners, a tough-looking bearded man in an orange tunic, can't contain himself. He lets out wild yells and howls, rushes on to the field, barges between the players to throw his arms around whichever of their boys has just kicked a goal.

The play comes barrelling past us, boys fighting to keep the ball alive, limbs and torsos and grimacing, gasping faces. Up close I can suddenly see the *purpose* that drives the tangle. It thrills me. Someone gets his boot to it and they're gone.

'You can hear the force in it, can't you,' says one of the fathers, rather faintly, 'when they come this close.'

Final quarter. Someone's down. Who is it? One of theirs. He's not getting up. He's not moving. Adults run to him. A strange human silence falls. Birds are singing, loudly. Each team draws back into its own ragged group. The sky is very high above the little circle of kneeling men. Behind them, the red-brown Sherrin lies on the grass, exactly halfway between the teams, as if positioned for a formal photo. A man jogs on to the ground carrying a translucent plastic stretcher. It takes the men several minutes to get the injured boy arranged on it. And they carry him off. All around the ground, a thin sprinkling of hand-claps: a salute to a fallen warrior.

'Highlight of the year,' says a Manor Lakes supporter to his mate, at the final siren. 'We only lost by four goals.'

———

The poor kid on the stretcher: ankle. No more info available.

———

Before training tonight I find Amby hunched over the kitchen table with a plastic bag of ice in his hand and a second bag clenched between shoulder and ear, against his neck. My concern, expressed in the least intrusive tone possible, in fact almost timidly, he rebuffs with a grunt.

A brilliant cold night, air so clear that the lights on the tunnel construction site blaze an unnaturally lurid yellow. Archie's parents come by with their dog. We lean side by side on the rail, watching, admiring. His dad tells us about a poet he's come across on the internet: 'Stevie Smith! "Not Waving but Drowning"! She's hilarious! Have you heard of her?'

'Actually,' I say, 'she's pretty famous.'

'To tell the truth, I was looking for Steve Smith, the cricketer.'

We hang over the rail in a fit.

Meanwhile, our boys are playing match sim. I can't make out what Archie is shouting, but his parents can.

'Did you hear that?' says his dad. 'He said, "Okay, what was wrong with that last kick? What was the mistake Amby made?" They have to analyse. Then the very next kick was perfect! And he said, "*That's* it! *That's* what I want to happen!" I think he might be a good coach! What's Amby carrying?'

'Jarred fingers. He got a hit in the neck, too, yesterday. And I think his legs are sore. He won't tell me if I ask.'

'Mmmm. General soreness.'

Off he goes with their dog, round the field in the dark to watch their daughter coaching her team. Archie's mum and I stay put. She is a school counsellor (as well as the sort of neighbour who'll come over to your place in her bee suit if yours are swarming and you don't know what to do)—so we can talk psychology.

'Shame,' she says. 'Shame was how older men used to be taught. It's baked into them. They can't help it. They pass it on down: "You were playing really well until you mucked it up just before the siren."'

'What do they think will go wrong, if they praise someone? Is it like that thing Hemingway said: *Praise to the face is open disgrace?*'

'Did you get praised,' she says, 'in your family?'

'No. Did you?'

'Yes.'

'I'm a generation older than you.'

Training ends. Amby gets into the car.

'Did you redeem yourself?'

'No.'

We drive home without speaking. Anything I say will grate on his nerves. He is sore all over. Inside and out.

—

Next day he brings home a sheet of paper with the high-school crest on it: an award. Signed by the principal.

'Gimme that thing. "For Outstanding Academic Growth".'

What? This bludger? Who drags the chain with homework? Who plays gruesome dark games on the big TV in the kitchen, his shoulders bowed over his phone? Who sings along word-perfect to endless rap on Spotify?

His whole vibe is transformed; his shoulders are back, his

head high, his face once more full of light.

'So! You *have* redeemed yourself!'

'No! Oh well, actually—yes. Not in footy, but because of the award.'

'So you're set for the week?'

'I am!' He hugs me against his brick-like abs and runs me through a couple of tries at a dap: 'You gotta loosen up! *Relax!*'

—

After training tonight the U18s are supposed to play a one-hour practice match against the Flemington Seniors. Amby wants to stay back and watch. But the U18s are unexpectedly a few men short. Four boys from the U16s are selected to make up the numbers: Luis, Angus, Fitzy and Amby—plus Archie for good measure. OMG. The U18s are scary enough but the Seniors are actual adult *men*. They've got barrel chests and great big hairy legs, some of them have full-on long beards. Before Amby runs on he bends over his backpack and takes a quick puff of ventolin.

It's a case of 'the Assyrian came down like a wolf on the fold'—the Seniors are fast, impatient and scornful, giving no quarter. I am the only person watching, in the cold and dark. I can almost feel their heavier frames, the greater density of their muscle, the massive wall of their adult bulk. I cringe behind the rail, pressing my back against a tree trunk. But our boys show no fear. They fight for that ball. They take good marks, they tackle like there's no tomorrow.

And an hour later, while the Seniors and the U18s troop away home along the Metro Tunnel boundary, our little group walks quietly off the field in the opposite direction, shoulder to shoulder with their coach, heading back to their innocent teenage backpacks and bikes. They don't even know I'm there, but I have to bite my lip not to shout their names with pride.

—

Eight am on a school morning and no sign of Amby. I tap on his door and call out. He answers. I go in: and there, sprawled on his back on a boy's single bed with its boy's orange and white doona flung back, lies a six-foot man, naked but for a pair of short cotton pyjama pants, his surfer's legs covered in golden hair, and a torso as flat and smooth and muscled as a goddamn model's. I'm stopped in my tracks.

He looks up at me calmly, his hands folded under his head. I laugh and his face opens into a roguish smile. The chunky child I used to carry on my hip! Where has he gone? Where have the *years* gone?

'Get up. You'll be late. Do you need anything?'

'Nope.'

I am dismissed.

Luckily I've just done my eleven-minute kirtan kriya meditation, quietly in my room with the door shut, or I might have been devastated by this moment of transformation. And can this be what he was telling me, three nights ago when we pulled up beside the oval and he said to me, as he gathered his things and fought the passenger door open, 'Thanks for dropping me off.'

Dropping me off? Hello? In future am I to drop him off before training and pick him up after it, rather than hanging around on my own in the dark with my notebook and pencil, offering my presence and my attention and my service where they are no longer needed? My willpower hardens. I am in this for the long haul, my fine fellow. You will not shake me off until the season is over.

—

I drive us to Point Cook. Amby navigates; his dad and the dog doze in the back seat. En route Amby checks his phone.

'Meth's not playing.'

'Is it his knee, still?'

'No. Says here he's "deathly sick".'

'Does he actually say *deathly*?'

'Yes.'

We are half an hour early, which his dad forbears to point out is caused by my anxiety about being late. Fine rain sprinkles and mists. We stand around on the boundary.

Two other Colts fathers stroll up. The three men launch into a conversation about the game played at the MCG the night before, a discussion so technical as to render me redundant. How relaxing this is—the tension goes out of me. I can sit back in the armchair of ignorance and listen to them happily comparing insights, opinions, memories of long-ago grand finals: 'Eighty-nine. Wasn't that the one where Dipper played on with a punctured lung?' 'I think it was Dipper.' 'Yeah, it was Dipper.' I am socially freed by their expertise. No one's going to ask anything of me. The light rain stops. I fold my big umbrella and hang it by its handle on the fence.

Amby's dad murmurs away as the game rolls on. 'One thing about Amby—when he gets the ball he always takes a bounce. That's a really good sign. And he plays better on pure instinct. I'd always put him in the guts.'

'The guts?'

'Midfield. As a forward you have to think too much.'

Three-quarter time and Silas's dad is out there among the team, squirting Griptek on their palms.

'Come in, lads, come in,' says Archie in a low, urgent voice. 'We got twenty more minutes. We can beat this team. We're gonna fuckin' kill 'em. Every one of us is gonna kill 'em.'

Amby's in the ruck. Again and again he goes up, hair flying, arms high, fingers spread. Every time he does something good we look at each other: 'Amby! That was Amby!'—as if we can't believe he's become so strong and tall. Amby the footballer has become someone I don't know—his bravery, his powerful concentration.

The Colts lose by seven points. One by one the boys emerge from the rooms to their parents, filthy, flushed, still staring-eyed with adrenalin. Amby strolls out, calmly, in white socks and Birkenstocks, carrying his boots and bag. He, his dad and I walk to the car.

'Want something to eat?'

He shakes his head. As he's opening the passenger door he says, so quietly that I almost don't hear him, 'I got best on ground.'

'You? Best on ground?'

He nods, restraining a smile.

'Oh, you little ripper. Bloody good on you. Congratulations.'

He laughs, dropping his face: 'Thanks, Hel.'

His dad praises him warmly, technically. I reverse out of the carpark and drive off towards the freeway. No one is speaking, but our car is hardly touching the road.

'I need water,' he says. 'I forgot to bring any.'

I pull into a tiny shopping strip, dash into a Lebanese food shop and seize a bottle from the fridge. The girl behind the counter smiles at me. How handsome she is in her dark hijab, how noble her pure skin and gracious manner! I can hardly hold back from saying, 'My grandson's thirsty! He's best on ground!'

Between swigs and guzzles of the water he says, 'Their ruckman called me *bitch*. He called me *pussy*. He said, "You can't take physical contact." Finally I tackled him and spun him around and *sssssat* him down. After that I was a bit scared, because he was a big, tough bogan.'

Back home, his dad goes out into the garden and continues to feed pruned branches into the mulcher. Amby and I sit on the couch to rest. His brother passes through the room, looking for his guitar.

'Hey. I got best on ground.'

'Awesome.'

'*And*,' I say, 'he got called pussy and bitch by their *ruckman*.'

His brother pauses at the door. 'Did you hit him?'

'No. But I smoked him, in the actual game.'

'Well done.'

Amby lays one long hairy leg across my lap.

'That guy who called you bitch,' I say. 'What did he look like? Was he bigger than you?'

'Yes. He was extremely buff. Spent a lot of time in the gym.'

'What sort of haircut?'

'A curly mullet. He wanted to get in a fight.'

'Got any injuries I should be attending to? Seeing your mum's in Canberra?'

'No. Everything's okay. Except I've got some nicks and scratches, that's all, and this old cut on my knee's opened up again. It's bleeding. Oh, and I've got these on my—well, I can't show you—'

'What?'

'I can't show you!'

'May I remind you that I have seen and personally scrubbed clean, at least a hundred times, every inch of your *famous body*? Come on. Show me.'

'I can't! It's too high!'

'Okay, put this cushion over the rude bits and show me the leg part.'

He scrupulously arranges a cushion and part of his shorts over the sensitive bits, and reveals a dark red graze, consisting of three parallel strokes about two inches long, at the very top of his inner thigh. 'It's from his studs.'

'Did he kick you?'

'Yeah.'

'Arsehole.'

We watch *Trailer Park Boys* for half an hour, then I go into my house and have a little nap. Exhausted by spectacle, loyalty, pride and outrage.

—

Monday training, and on the way out the door at 5.45 he says, 'The light's weird. It's usually darker when we leave.'

'What'll happen tonight?'

'He'll make us run. I ran so far in the game yesterday I'm sore all over. He always makes us run if we lost, or if we played badly.'

'Is it a punishment?'

'No.'

At the oval it's almost dark, and the air is sweet. I don't want it to be spring—it's too early to be spring. Is this global warming? I sit on the high back of my bench, not expecting anything to happen that I haven't seen before.

Why do I like training so much? Helplessly concentrating on something I can hardly see, hardly make out in the dusk, way down at the other end? I like watching other people do things. It's time that I'm not in control of: it's got nothing to do with me. And yet they seem to be enacting something *in* me. Something I need to see played out. Sometimes what they're doing is almost abstract. Like a musician playing scales, working to get it right, to make it perfect: maybe this is what Remy's doing when he shouts, 'Again! Again! Again!'

Here comes Archie's mum. She pauses in her walk to do what all the footy parents like to do: praise each other's offspring.

'Amby was incredible yesterday, in the ruck,' she says. 'He jumped so high! He always has this joyful sort of spring. He's not scared to try things. I saw him playing in the sand hills, once. He was running and leaping—then he just threw himself into a backflip. Landed on his feet! I said, "How did you learn to do that?" He said, "I don't know. I just thought, I can probably do it, and it worked."'

Meanwhile this paragon is tearing across the grass with one arm outstretched bellowing, 'Meth! Jake! Fitzy! Harvey! Silas!' in his hoarse, mad-sounding voice.

Archie's mum strolls on. A low, hard, mechanical whirring bursts out of the dark behind me. I jump with fright. A kid with his black hood up shaves past me on a BMX bike, going like the clappers, rearing up on his back wheel so far that I wish he'd overdo it and crash, right in front of me, so I could watch his downfall, the little smartarse. But he jams on his brakes, throws a wheelie behind the goalposts, and settles there, coughing, both feet on the ground, just close enough to the boys to distract Angus, who's already drifting away from the action and wandering off between the goals.

Archie yells for Angus to come in and work. Angus casts over his shoulder a languid glance. I give the kid with the bike a dirty look. His hood is up but his face is visible in three-quarter profile. Our eyes meet. I nod severely. He smiles. He is only a child. With a cough like a dog's bark.

Training ends. The team shambles in. Angus is straggling, eyes on the ground.

Archie shouts, 'You do one more dickhead thing, Angus, and you'll run a lap.' Confused movements, a shove and a stumble. Archie's voice cuts through: 'Right. No one's going home till Angus has run a lap in eighty seconds.'

Groans and curses. Away he goes, anticlockwise, in his baggy white shorts and T-shirt, and soon he's only a thin, pale, long-limbed figure gliding smoothly way over there along the southern boundary, fast and steady in the dark; and as he rounds the curve behind the eastern goalposts, the boys in their cluster, crossly yanking off their boots and swigging from water bottles, turn as one towards the approaching runner and begin to shout for him: 'Go, Angus! Come on, Angus, come on!' All his teammates' voices calling his name—is this what he needs? Here he comes, along the northern boundary, blank-faced, no sign of haste or strain, in long, untiring strides—and yes! He's made it! A few sparse cheers. They can all go home.

Boys hurry towards their fathers' cars waiting along the fence. Motors turn over and headlights flick on. Angus ignores them, stoops to pick up a ball, and nonchalantly punts it through the big sticks into the dark.

Amby, this large tired creature, wedges himself into the passenger seat beside me.

'Thank God for adrenalin,' he says. 'If I didn't have adrenalin I'd be in so much pain all the time.'

'What were the dickhead things Angus was doing?'

'He had cupcakes.'

'What? Eating them? On the field?'

'Yeah.'

I start laughing feebly and can't stop. Amby looks out the window, bored, impassive, too knackered to care.

'Want to get something to eat? Will I stop at the supermarket?'

'Okay. We could get cupcakes.'

He stays in the shower for a long time. When we are called to the table, he takes his place and works his way with good appetite through the meal his dad has prepared. He's in a different world: he sits quietly while the rest of us talk and crack jokes, drinks a lot of water, clears the plates, thanks his dad for the food, and goes to bed.

—

On Saturday afternoon the Western Bulldogs verse Greater Western Sydney in Ballarat. We are ahead at half-time but we lose two defenders to injury (knee; concussion). GWS get rolling and thrash us. Toby Greene kicks goal after goal. Galling. Something about the shape of his head, like a tilted olive, and his vain little walk undermines my admiration for his dazzling play. And I don't know how to forgive or forget his past brutality.

Amby has his shift at Cheaper Buy Miles so his dad and I watch the game on our own, silently, in deepening gloom. After the siren I trudge into the backyard and yank a whole lot of ugly weeds out of the cracks in the paving. Amby is going to stay over at his friend Macca's place in Footscray tonight.

'Why don't you take your footy gear with you,' I say, 'and get the train straight to your game in the morning?'

'No. I'll come home first. I'll get up at eight. Because it's the team photo before the game. I need to look good.'

I laugh coarsely. 'What—bouffe up your mullet?'

'*No.*'

—

The photographer has the chairs set up in rows for the U14s, but by the time it's the U16s' turn the sun has moved and the angle of the light is wrong.

'They'll either be squinting,' he says, 'or there'll be a line right down the middle of their faces, one half dark, the other bright.'

He shifts operations to a yellow wall round the corner that's in full shade—the vertically ridged side of a shipping container that is part of the outer wall of a risk-taking adventure playground famous in our suburb as 'the Venny'.

'The kids'd come home from the Venny,' says Boof's mum, 'and you'd think, okay, every single thing they've got on goes straight into the washing machine, they'd be so filthy. And remember those little animals they had? What were they called?' We rack our brains and burst out in unison: '*Guinea pigs!*' She mimes holding a furry creature to her face and going coochy-coo.

Meth hasn't turned up. She texts him. They wait, on their three levels, all fresh-faced, scrubbed and shining, the shorter guys standing on chairs at the back, arms invisible; the middle row angled inwards, arms folded and fists thrust under biceps; the big ones sitting bare-thighed and manspreading in the front row, Remy holding a ball, the others with loose fists resting on their legs, knuckles forward, sportsman style. Remy looks as serious and serene as a bridegroom. Somebody calls out 'Socks!' They all look down. Oh *no*. Some have artfully crushed their socks down around their ankles, others are wearing them drawn up tight to show the yellow band. There's a bit of shouting and muttering: it's agreed (or someone orders) that they should be pulled up. Everyone adjusts. Next to my foot someone has trodden an orange mouthguard deep into the damp grass.

While we wait for Meth, the mothers murmur to each other. One says that her son has been coughing blood and will have to miss two games. 'He didn't want to tell Archie he couldn't play,' she says. 'He thought the others would think he was "soft".' We flinch and breathe in sharply.

Here comes Meth, racing across the park between the trees. He hasn't got his team jumper.

'There's a spare one in my bag,' says Boof's unflappable

mum. She describes to Meth the exact whereabouts of the spare, and off he dashes.

'Better Meth run for it than me,' she says, 'though I'm not too sure about a fifteen-year-old boy looking for something...'

'*Or* a man,' I say, and again we double up laughing. Amby's dad, only last night, had lost his wallet, last sighting at Dan Murphy, he turns the house upside down, calls the grog shop, rings the police station—'No,' he says, no point *me* looking, he's already searched everywhere. I say, 'Okay, but how about I take a quick glance around? Sometimes a fresh eye...' We stop at the doorway of their bedroom. He glances along the floor at the edge of the bed and there it is, half an inch into the shadowed, dusty area underneath.

'My husband,' says Boof's mum, 'couldn't find our TV remote. Anywhere. It had completely vanished. He was desperate. And he said, "Anybody who can find the remote gets a hundred dollars." One of the girls walked into the room and saw it right away.'

Meth comes tearing back with the jumper, drags it on, shuffles into position. I scan the rows: is someone else missing? It's Boof. He's already left for Darwin. There's a gap in the vibe where he should be.

The boys arrange their features, raise their chins. Ned, who officially plays for the Colts U14s but trains and plays an extra game with the U16s, is at the end of the back row, standing on a chair. His face is pale, he is fidgeting, putting both hands up to his temples, letting his head fall back, his eyebrows in an inverted V.

'Is Ned all right?' I say to his mum, who's standing next to me. 'He looks so white—is he sick?'

'Ah, no,' she says, in the pacific tone of a mother of teenage boys. 'He tends to get a bit panicky when he thinks he's going to be late. His actual team's playing at Altona. He's got plenty of time to get there.'

He calms himself and straightens his spine. Right in the middle of the second row, at the very heart of the photo, stands Angus, his earring flatly gleaming, his skin pale as wax, his hair cut short over his ears and with a fringe like Russell Crowe's in *Gladiator*. He faces the camera with a cheeky confidence.

The photographer lines up his shot. 'Ready?'

Their faces open. They are poised trembling on the cusp of manhood: they have no idea how beautiful they are. And before the photographer can take a breath, Angus shouts 'CHEESE!' and the whole tableau splinters and falls apart in laughter. Hasty reform, 'Cupcakes!' and the job is done. Ned leaps to the ground and takes off running in a westerly direc-tion. They shout after him, 'Good luck! Go Neddie! Don't forget to warm up!'

—

Restless early spring—at the end of *July*. A strong wind, from the north. I have to hold my hat on with both hands, from bounce to siren. Protect them, Lord, from injury. We beat PEGS by forty-three points.

—

Team pizza night after Monday training, which I miss for a family farewell to a traveller. Amby trudges up the hill from the ground to the party. He arrives beaming, carrying two leftover pizzas in their boxes. He's whacked, and sore. After we've all sung 'Wish Me Luck as You Wave Me Goodbye' and everyone's settling in to drinking and laughing, he needs to go home. In the car he examines a series of red marks on his thigh.

'Are those from that same ruckman who kicked you?'

'No. They're new ones, from yesterday.'

'A friend of mine,' I say, 'told me about visiting a family whose son plays for the Saints. He walked through the room in shorts and no shirt. His whole body was covered in bruises. They're scars of battle, aren't they.'

'Yes.'

'Do you feel proud of them?'

'Yes.'

'Why?'

'Because they show that I've been…out there. That people have done things to me. And that I could survive it.'

'Were you best on ground?'

'No. Jake was best, then Luis, then me. And Helen—guess what. The team needs a third captain, for the finals.' He drops his voice. 'And it's me.'

He is incredulous, jubilant. 'When they announced it,' he says, all flushed and grinning, 'I had to get up and say some words.' But he's worried that it might be 'a bit of favouritism', because Archie's family and ours know each other.

'Favouritism? I don't think so,' says his dad, when everyone gets home. 'The family connection would have been more likely to stop Archie from favouring you. Archie's an honourable guy.'

So it's Remy, Jake and Ambrose. Remy is a born leader, a thinker, a shouter. Jake is acknowledged as the team's most naturally gifted player, and he's what they call ultra-competitive—maybe he instigates the fights that Angus can't resist getting into? The vice captain is Boof, but he's in Darwin.

I ask Amby what a third captain actually does.

'I'm not exactly sure. Say encouraging words?'

Maybe the team needs another bellowing boy. Maybe Amby this season has grown into one. He's taller and heavier and louder, his game is way more aggressive, he shows no fear. And listening to him and his dad when we watch games on TV, I see that he also has a sense of tactics.

August

Oh, this sweet air!—after a frighteningly early spring day of 19°C. I want to fill my lungs with it. Soft pink clouds in wandering streaks, as night falls. Soon there'll be a moon. Ten minutes later the breeze freshens and cools, I'm glad of my jacket. I'm *waiting* for the moon.

'Point your toes, boys!' shouts Archie. 'Make sure we're *loud* here, boys! Look wide, look wide! Good give!'

I love to see a player snatch the ball and break into that graceful run, veering inwards from the boundary, smoothly and regularly bouncing, in full command.

Two non-footy guys in their thirties run past on the thick grass near my boundary possie. Something odd in their gait: they raise their knees high, like prancing ponies. Oh, I get it—they're barefoot. Their feet meet the ground so light and delicate, they seem hardly to press the grass.

Somebody's calling, 'Angus!' Three younger boys on bikes cluster on the path in the dark, further round the rail. Angus

ambles away from the team to talk to them. They run him
through the dap routine. I expect a shout from Archie but he's
busy elsewhere, and maybe he's given up trying to get Angus
to concentrate.

Angus wanders back to the drill and they all draw into a
rough circle, yelling what sounds like 'FUCK FUCK FUCK!'
Is it a fight? A protest? No, they're laughing, milling about,
ready to play a match sim against the U18s who, over on the
southern side, are pulling on their orange vests, which make
them look better organised, more team-like, more lethal.

White gulls circle idly, and the game begins.

Faithfully I watch, faithfully I pay my confused and
amateurish attention. Where's the moon? Why am I here,
crouching in the dark on the back of a bench near a skate
park? Is it grandiose to remember the poem that talks about
'love's austere and lonely offices'? I need the moon. Where *is*
it? Just as match sim ends and the boys tramp off the field
to their pile of backpacks, I turn towards my car and see it,
in the bottom right-hand corner of my vision: an immense,
fat, crinkly-edged, pinkish-orange balloon, rolling up from
behind the screen of still-bare elm branches—nowhere near
the piece of sky in which I'd been expecting to see it, waiting
for it to rise and shine down upon us, and bless us.

'Boys,' shouts Archie as they gather up their bags. 'Don't go
out Saturday night. Stay home. Just that one night.'

In the car: 'Did you see me?'

'I did! You were going great guns!'

'Did you see my marks?'

'Yes!'

'Did you see my tackles!'

'Yes!'

'I just need,' he says, apparently satisfied, 'to do more work on my goal-kicking. I've kicked too many points this season. At the end of match sim tonight the U18s' coach said to us, "Good luck for your match on Sunday—and good luck to whoever's on Ambrose!"'

'He said *that*?'

'Yeah. And everyone was like, "*Woh hoh*, Ambrose!" and ruffled my hair.'

—

A Friday night. The Bulldogs are versing Richmond, but Amby's dad's band is playing at Kindred in Footscray, so we won't be watching. On the drive over, Amby, his mum and I agree to remain in ignorance till we can get home and watch the whole game. But my sister texts me: 'Wonderful Dogs!' In a dark corner of the bar Amby and I furtively check the scores on his phone. They're looking good. We settle in with a negroni for me and a soda lime and bitters for him.

'No one I know,' I say, 'is likely to be at this gig.'

'You and me both, Hel.'

He shows me how to use the Notes app on my phone.

'A lot of people,' I say, 'have the Western Bulldogs as their second team.'

'They're a charming team.'

'Yeah, and decent. Not composed of thugs, or reformed thugs.'

The band starts to play and I rush down to dance with Amby's mum and a bunch of neighbours from our street who have unexpectedly turned up. Amby joins the wall of standing men behind the dancers.

An hour or so in, back at our corner, I say, 'As a footballer in training, would you be likely to want to go home early?'

'Yes, I would.'

'Okay. I won't drink any more.'

He points to the dregs of my single negroni: 'Want me to finish that?'

'No. It's powerful.'

'*I* am powerful.'

I grab the drink and smash it back, just in case. I am introduced by our neighbour, a Zumba-mad, cricket-tragic psych nurse, to her colleague, a cool young social worker in a knitted beanie. Beanie girl and I take a shine to each other and exchange tales of psychologically and spiritually meaningful incidents we have witnessed in footy.

'Sport,' she declares, raising her glass, 'is *sacred*.'

'A truer word was never spoken.'

Meanwhile Amby's dad, wearing a white Stetson and carrying a nine-iron across his shoulders, has with his band transformed a quiet crowd into a packed mass of prancing, laughing, singing nutcases. Amby and I, our minds on sacred things, regretfully take our leave.

I drive the Corolla up the steep side street to the road home.

At the top of the hill I turn right and encounter a bewilder-
ingly complicated series of lanes and arrows. A car appears
way down at the bottom, near the river, heading up the slope
towards us, headlights blazing.

'Hel,' says Amby calmly. 'Move into the other lane. Left.
Hel. You're on the wrong side of the road. Get into the *left*.'

The pattern of white lines sinks in.

'My GOD.' With a skilful if slightly frantic swoop of the
wheel I correct our trajectory and we proceed in an easterly
direction. The other car, heading west, approaches smoothly
and passes without incident. We cross the river in silence.

'Maybe I should give up night driving.'

'I can ride my bike to training.'

'*Nooooooooo*,' I cry, mortified. 'The evenings are already
getting lighter.'

When we get home Amby and his brother have the cheek
to correct my 'funny' way of peeling a mandarin. Apparently
these days one pokes one's thumb into the bottom of the fruit,
rather than the top where the stalk was, as I have been doing
for seventy-five years. Thanks, boys. Who knew?

—

I wake on the morning of our game against Point Cook
surprised to find I'm almost sick with nerves. Amby is going
to be on the same ruckman as last time we played this team,
the one who called him bitch and pussy and kicked him.
Amby grits his teeth and scowls: this time, he says, he's going

to fight. What if he gets really hurt?

For the drive down the Princes Highway I insist ('because I'm the smallest') upon climbing into the very rear of the van, practically the boot, where there's a tiny collapsible seat. Not even the dog wants it. He leaps over the seatback and squeezes in between Amby's brother and sister. I feel silly about my fit of false humility, but it's too late now, and actually there's something cosy about my spot. It's rather private. I think I'll try for it next time too.

On the road Amby's dad plays various versions of the Vanda and Young song 'Evie'. The one with the guitar solo, so dated and so powerfully emotional, makes me think he's using music to back Amby without having to speak—to put heart into him.

At the ground there's a big crowd. The carpark is packed. There's a fast turnover: when a team comes off at the end of their game they have to cool their heels outside the rooms while the next team finishes singing their revving-up song and rushes past them to play. Our families stand around humbly, waiting to see the boys come charging out.

'Are you nervous? I am!' says Silas's dad. The boy whose mum told me at the photo shoot that he had been coughing blood comes hurrying out in street clothes, one hand up to his face. Out pour the others: the hulking walk, even if you're not a hulk; the walk of men with shoulders.

'Has Amby been in the gym?' says Meth's mum in her whispery way. 'Look at his *arms*!'

'No! I keep telling him he should but he won't!'

We are almost giggling with nerves. Everyone around us is carrying on melodramatically about Collingwood's young star Nick Daicos and his broken leg.

I mutter under my breath, 'Oh, I don't care.'

Silas's grandmother is shocked: 'We *should* care. He's young. They give their bodies.'

Shamed, I look at the ground.

The Colts race away in the first quarter. If we were kicking straight we'd already have four goals—and yet we're surging, flying—we're everywhere. Amby's feared opponent in the ruck is playing fair: he's good, a tall, strong boy, with nothing grotesque in the haircut department. Up they go each time, one arm high to tap the ball, nothing dirty going on—I can stop worrying and hating. Two long-haired teenage girls crouch on a low bench, stuffing food into their faces as they keenly follow the progress of the game. They stiffen at the sound of the whistle. The umpire gives a free against Flemington. '*Whaaaaat?*' cries one of the girls, her hamburger poised before her gaping mouth. 'Are you fucking *joking*?' We win, 58:26.

—

All the next day a strange thought keeps coming to me: I don't know if I'm worthy. Worthy of *what*? Of their tremendous life force. I draw on it. I'm even living off it.

I get home from work ten minutes later than usual, though still in plenty of time to get Amby to training on the dot.

But he's ridden his bike to the ground. He's a captain now. He'd rather ride there in the dark and cold than hang around waiting for me and risk turning up late. Never in his life has he shown this degree of faithfulness to duty.

I drive down there and take up my spot. A brief burst of clapping from the tight ring of boys out in the centre of the field before they start work. Match sim in the dark. The voices shouting for the ball, howling for it. Remy's tremendous, deep-chested roar. I'm cold. I'm shivering, perched on the high back of my bench. I'm even glancing at my watch, but I don't want it to end. I want it to go on forever, to be near it forever.

Driving home I ask Amby what the clapping was about.

'Three guys,' he says, not looking at me, 'have been invited to try out for the Calder Cannons. It's a feeder team for the AFL.'

'Who were the three?'

'Remy, Jake and Josh.'

'Not you?'

'Not me.'

'Are you disappointed, Amb?'

'Yes.'

He does not complain, but he is silent all the way home.

—

Wednesday night. I walk into the kitchen next door. Amby's dad is cooking. Amby is hugely standing around, leaning on things. No one else is present. There is an unusual, almost breathless silence in the room, as if I've intruded on something personal. Amby digs his finger into my shoulder, a sign of good humour, though he doesn't say anything. I glance up at him. He gives me a slanted smile and raises his eyebrows.

'What's going on?'

'Has Helen heard your—'

'No.'

'Show her.'

Amby hands me his dad's phone. On its screen appears the following exchange:

How tall is Ambrose
181cm we just measured him
OK 5'11" I'll see what I can do
Thanks Rob He's a competitor

'Who's Rob?'

'Another spotter.'

Seconds later, a text from Archie pings into Amby's phone:

Would you have any interest in Calder

Amby towers there in front of the fridge, rigid with self-control. He texts back:

I would

From the table I say, 'Can I write all this in my notebook?'

'Yes.'

'Read it out to me.'

When he gets to the text from Archie I say, 'Is there a question mark?'

'No. People don't use question marks in texts.'

'Oh, don't be ridiculous.'

'They don't!'

'Why? Is it uncool or something?'

'They're just not necessary.'

Eddie Betts came through the Calder Cannons. So did Mitch Wallis. Tom Liberatore. Rhylee West. I'm terrified of injury. I don't know how parents stand it. And Amby's dad describes in the most sickening detail (twice, because he thinks we didn't understand it the first time) Mitch Hannan's ruptured Achilles. We have to ask him to stop.

After the pasta and the clearing of dishes I move towards the door. Amby and his father seem to be connected across the room by an invisible thread, or force field. They need me not to be there. So I make myself scarce.

—

Time to leave for training. I appear at his bedroom door. He's rolled in his doona.

'Come on.'

'I forgot to tell you. My coach is going to be late.'

'Who?'

'My coach.'

'My coach? I *know* your coach, dingbat.'

'Okay. Archie. He's going to be late so we don't need to leave yet.'

'Thanks a lot for telling me.'

—

Thick grey cloud cover. It's almost dark. The klieg lights are blinding me. I forgot my hat. It's already cooling. I forgot my gloves. The boys pound past me in a squad on their warm-up run, talking in quiet voices. The one who was coughing blood is back on deck. Do I come to training because I need a reason to be in the park at dusk? To see night fall? The trains go smashing past on the raised line. I'm doing nothing more than being present. Maybe there's value in that.

A thin man with a neat little pack on his back pedals up. He props his pushbike against a post and comes to lean beside me at the rail. He introduces himself: Fitzy's dad, a GP and the club's chief trainer. We gossip for a moment about mushrooms, and marvel at the poisoning drama that's unfolding down at Korumburra. He gives me a textbook description of the kind of broken leg he imagines the young Collingwood star Nick Daicos has sustained. He's come this evening to check out any injuries.

'Round this time of the season,' he says, 'the soft tissue injuries start to make themselves felt.'

One of the boys trots over, greets him with a smile, and reports on his recent discomforts.

'Do you feel you can play a quarter? You won't be able to go in as hard as you usually do.'

'I sprinted the other night,' says the boy stoutly, 'and I was okay.'

'All right. You can play deep. See how you go.'

Off he jogs, back to the drills.

'What's "deep"?'

'Forward, or back. Not midfield.'

'Did you play footy as a boy?'

He laughs. 'I've never played. I was in the chess club at school. But I love footy. We follow Essendon. And with these boys'—he gestures towards the yelling Colts executing their rapid handball patterns—'I like to be near them.'

Near them. So it's not just me.

I look up from our conversation and see an alarming sight on the far side of the ground: eighteen guys in orange vests massing in the dimness, facing our way. It's the U18s. There's going to be a match sim. The U16s on the boundary near us are stripping off their T-shirts and jumpers and turning them inside out. Their triangular torsos are winter ivory—smooth, youthful muscle.

An hour later, while they're pulling on their home clothes, Archie revs them up for their coming match against the dreaded Newport. I can't hear what he's saying but I see them jostling tightly around him, letting out the odd cry or shout. Just before they part till Sunday, Remy calls for silence and declares in stentorian tones: 'Boys! It's not about the number on the back. It's about the emblem on the front.'

I can hardly hold in my laughter. I admire them. I am devoted to them. That's why I'm here.

On the drive home Amby reports, looking carefully neutral, what Archie had told him: that the scout from Calder Cannons had asked him, 'Is Ambrose any good? He played well at Point Cook. He's got a great leap, and God, he's strong.'

Whatever else happens, Amby will rejoice to the end of his days over 'God, he's strong'.

—

The Newport ground on Sunday has a noisy, festive air, almost like a party. Families are out in force: women in hijab and long coats, swathed in slanting, fluttering lengths of cloth; bare-ankled men in tight-calved black tracksuits and little round skullcaps. There's a genial irreverence in their demeanour. On a poster encouraging volunteering some joker has scribbled *The umpires a pedo.* Every mark gets loud praise, the merest behind a cheer; the parents look around to share their delight.

How quiet our team's supporters are! We stand there like inner-city intellectuals, analysing our boys, criticising their every move, using modal verbs in knuckle-rapping tenses: *should have, ought to have.*

'We've kicked really really badly all day,' says Amby's dad. 'Normally we're pretty good by foot but we're just not handling the pressure. They're giving us no breathing space at all. Ninety-five per cent of our kicks have been shit.'

Why haven't we all brought our families out here with us? It's only thirty minutes west of where we live. Why aren't we a mob, shouting for our boys, whistling, calling out encouragement, instead of muttering our disappointments? They need to hear our love and loyalty, our belief in them, out there on the hard, dry ground, facing up to the heavier-bodied, tactically smart, mostly Middle-Eastern boys who today, in spite of our bravery and desperate application, mark strongly, kick straight and overwhelm us 10.4 (64) to 2.10 (22).

Meanwhile, down in Tasmania, the Western Bulldogs are busy losing to Hawthorn by three points.

'Typical,' says Amby's dad, shoving his phone into his pocket. 'They do this every bloody time. What a crap day of footy.'

I make a squeaky little attempt to arrest his slump into gloom, despair and contempt: 'It doesn't prove anything, you know.'

'Well, it does actually.'

'Not in the universe.'

'Maybe not in the universe. But it's a game the Dogs *should've* won. By eight points at least.'

We plod on to the ground to stand near our boys. The two teams group and face each other again for the formalities of victory and defeat, a custom I love and regard always with a deep sense of rightness. When I see the Newport players advancing towards ours in a V-shaped bloc I quail for a second, as at the approach of a regiment, but their captain and coach are smiling graciously. I know it wasn't a violent or dirty game. They have simply outplayed us. In the handshake line I am proud to see Amby and the big, chafing-thighed Newport forward who tremendously kicked most of their goals make full-faced, sparkly eye contact, and even laugh.

Outside the rooms, waiting for the demolished Colts to turn back into ordinary kids who want to go home, their former coach, Tommy and Ned's dad, says to me phlegmatically, 'It's always like this, with U16s. The Middle-Eastern boys develop earlier. At this age they're already more like men. In a year or so our boys will have built up a greater weight of muscle, and the Middle-Eastern guys will no longer have that advantage.'

We give Liam a lift back to Newmarket station. Amby's dad finds it in his heart to praise him: 'Your cross-body kick to Remy was very good.' Shy Liam, in the back seat with Amby, makes no reply, or if he does, I don't hear it. I'm remembering three Newport dads I saw under a tree, when we arrived at the ground, standing quietly with their backs to the field, then kneeling side by side on a little mat, their hands held out palms up in a gesture of appeal or acceptance.

Amby and his dad must have been engaged in a densely analytical post-game colloquium while I messed around in my house, for by the time I take my half-bottle of wine into their kitchen at dinner time, Amby is talking to a friend on his phone, his dad (Bulldogs beanie pompom bobbing on his head) is energetically peeling potatoes to go with the roast pork, and the vibe is bouncy. Amby's dad lays out for me their plan for the Colts. I see at once that it makes sense—that is, I grasp his point. Maybe I'm not as thick about footy as I think I am.

The problem is, he says, that none of our forwards are natural extroverts. 'They're all contributors, and they all have their days, but there's no big personality down there running the show and demanding the ball week in, week out.' What we need, he says, is a permanent forward who's a commanding presence, like for example Remy—a lighthouse they can all kick towards. Remy could be to the forward line what Boof is to the back line. Meanwhile Angus can go to the ruck when Amby needs a rest; he's got the right competitive streak and he's tall and athletic enough for the job. He can move forward again whenever it's necessary.

At least, I *think* that's what he says. I imagine that in every Colts kitchen in the suburb a family is coming up with its own tactical brainwave.

That night I get a text from the coach's mum. 'Arch,' she writes, 'is stunned and mystified about the game.'

—

Amby's mum is in Canberra again, finishing her research fellowship. Amby's ears have been blocked for a week or so. We assumed it was a wax build-up, and I keep dripping Waxsol into them, to no avail. His dad reckons we ought to get some ear candles. I google them. They sound a bit fishy. I get him a doctor's appointment for Monday before school.

The GP takes one look into his ears with his little pointy gadget and says, 'There's no wax. Your eardrums are all red. It's a middle ear infection. Well established.'

Guiltily I buy the antibiotics and a nasal spray, and drop him at school with his medical certificate. At lunchtime I text him a reminder to take the second pill. He doesn't answer.

I get home late in the afternoon. Soon it will be time to go to training. Music issues from behind his closed bedroom door. I tap and enter. He's lying in his school uniform on top of his bed.

'Is everything all right?'

'Yes,' he says tonelessly.

'Did you take the pill?'

'Yes.'

'Are you going to training?'

'Yes.'

'What's the matter?'

He rears up off the pillow, his face dark and focused, exactly as it is when he's playing. 'Nothing. *Nothing. NOTHING'S CHANGED.*'

Shocked, I kick the door and stamp back into my house. Get yourself to training, then. What if I tell him to ride his bloody bike? But he might get knocked off it in traffic in the dark and it would be my fault for sulking. My amour-propre deflates with a long, slow, audible hiss. Who do I think I am, intruding on his privacy, feeding off his life, trying to *write a book* about it?

I go gloomily about my household tasks, the chooks, the washing that's only half dry. I am once again what I've always been: a very small piece of shit, and furthermore, now, an old one, lonely, sad, ugly, garrulous, a nuisance, a bore.

In twenty minutes he calls me from the hall, ready to go. On the drive to the ground he says, 'I think the season's exactly the right length. It ends just when you're starting to get sick of it. And then after a while you start craving it—you don't know how to get rid of your...'

'Anger?'

'Maybe.'

'Why did you shout at me, back then?'

'What?'

'Why did you shout at me?'

He sighs. 'I never know whether you've got your hearing aids in or not. And I had a bad day at school. Sorry. Sorry for shouting.'

'All right. It's okay.'

We pull up on Kensington Road at 5.45. No one else is here. The sky holds a faint tinge of pink, misty yet somehow pure. Foliage is still spiky and bare.

'It's cold. If you notice I'm not here, I'll be back at 7.30.'

'I never notice whether you're here or not.'

This is what I've wanted, right from the first training, back in February—it's what I *thought* I wanted, and bragged about having—the invisibility of the witness. When he whacks it down like that, though, it stings. He hops out in silence and slopes away. When I get my breath back I slink to my spot on the rail, at a decent distance from the team.

It's as good as dark. The next field, the soccer one, is blazing white, but our big lights aren't on yet. The cold inserts its blade between glove and cuff. Where is everyone?

Wait—there's Aidan, pacing diagonally across the darkening field. Archie, tall in his loose white hoodie, steps out of his work van, lugging sacks of gear. Here comes the boy who looks like Remy but smaller, is it Antonio?—and Remy himself bounds over the gutter, swinging a black bag, his neck drastically shaved below his dark, curly crop: the opposite of a mullet.

They manifest from every direction, not in a hurry,

walking steadily and faithfully, or scooting, or pedalling, or scrambling out of their parents' cars. As they gather, Archie taps each boy's hand. They form into a loose circle around him. A sudden whiff of liniment. Archie's voice, sharp and serious. They share a solemn purpose. They are committed to it. It's boys' business. And my job is to witness it.

—

On the Tuesday morning before the preliminary final I wake from a shallow sleep and find a text from Archie that I missed in the night. It's about Boof. As the finals loom, Boof's heart, in the Northern Territory, turns faithfully south to his mates in the Colts. And it's mutual: ever since he went away there's been a Boof-shaped hole in the side—not only in its game, but in its spirit, its sense of itself as a team. Boof is the guy you want next to you in the trenches. But he's not here. And now his dad has forwarded to Archie a text from Boof in Darwin:

Book the tickets
Jake's not confident
Get me down there
I'm coming home

He will arrive at 11.40 on Saturday night and leave again for Darwin at 6.40 Sunday evening.

Archie is beside himself. 'He loves his mates so much that he'd come back for literally nineteen hours to help them win!'

—

Very cold tonight at training: clouded and dim. I watch for a while, but dreamily. Between drills and for no apparent reason somebody drops his shorts and flashes his arse, two perfect dead-white globes. No one seems to notice, or if they do they ignore it. Amby trains with desperate vigour and grit. He *will not give way.* If he goes for the ball and misses, he goes for it again, and again, turns, fights off opponents, dashes away, bouncing it, shoulders hunched, hair flying.

I get cold and retreat to the car, missing the match sim with the U18s. Eventually Amby bursts into the car, all joyful, and shows me his cut knee, a juicy wound with blood running down his hairy shin and calf.

'Guess what! You know my crush? Well, her brother plays in the U18s, and her dad's their assistant coach. He was umpiring. And just before the bounce—he was holding the ball—her dad said to me, "Are you Ambrose? Heard a lot about you! Good to meet you at last!" And he shook my hand!' He throws his head back in a fit of crazed laughter.

Back in the kitchen I stand him against a wall so I can take a photo of the bleeding wound to send to his mum. He's still wearing short white socks and Birkenstocks. It's a bad look, we agree. I make him take off the sandals.

'How did you get the cut?'

'In a tackle on Kang.'

'Who's Kang?'

'He's a kid at school. The tackle was fair. My knee scraped the floor.'

(He always says 'the floor' rather than 'the ground'.)

His dad sends us to Racecourse Road for some Turkish bread. When we walk past the Doutta Galla, Amby lays his arm across my shoulders in a relaxed manner, I put mine around his waist and we pace along like that, like friends, comfortable and pleasant. It makes me think of the time when he was barely even a toddler and I had the ludicrous idea that I could carry him on my hip into the city on the train. I'd thought of him as tiny but within a hundred metres he was a great lump of a thing. We met our neighbour near the mouth of the underpass and she flatly told me I was nuts. I didn't want to turn back. We rounded the bend and saw an abandoned pusher lying on its side in the tunnel. 'There's your pram, Helen,' said our neighbour in her mocking way. I stood it up and plonked him into it, and on we rolled to the station.

Walking home tonight with the bread I tell him my thoughts about the quietness of the Colts supporters at the Newport game. I ask him if they care, if they actually even hear the spectators when they are playing. He says no: 'When you've got the ball and you're on a big run down the field, you're concentrating so hard on bouncing it, and scanning the whole field as you run, looking for a target, checking whether anyone's coming up behind you, that you don't hear anything at all.'

'And do you feel it, as a player, the moment when your team loses heart and begins to fall apart?'

'Yes. You can feel it. You stop being able to trust that people will be where you need them to be.'

—

Early on the morning of preliminary final day I wake among the shards of a bizarre dream: I was in Paris, walking along an avenue, and I saw—

I sit bolt upright in my bed. Is it a prediction? A portent? Oh no! I can't possibly tell anyone about this. What if I told, and it made them lose?

At breakfast time next door I find a minor crisis in progress. Amby's brother, who had been at a party the night before, has just fainted in the bathroom. Twice. He is now sitting on the couch, rather subdued, beside his sensible girlfriend. While we're asking all the right questions, Amby is somewhere else, afloat in his private world. He stands at the kitchen bench, making himself a coffee and singing along to the Flamingos' doo-wop version of 'I Only Have Eyes for You'.

I turn to the sports pages of the Sunday *Age* and out leaps a terrifying photo: Carlton's 'spearhead', the famously sweet-faced, curly-headed Charlie Curnow, who the day before, in a game against Gold Coast, had 'put the Blues on his back' and 'carried them over the line himself'. I stare at the photo in horror: his massive head in profile rearing back, neck rigid and jaw clenched, and his bare right arm, bulging with muscle and sinew and disproportionately tremendous, brandishing in triumph a club-like fist. It's Homeric: all the ugly brutality of a raging Achilles, but also this strange and splendid beauty.

After breakfast I sneak away to the internet and watch the game's final moments. Curnow emerges out of a contest in the goal square with the impossible mark that saves his side—his kick is perfect, the crowd goes berserk—and he lowers his head, grips it in both hands, and drops forward to the ground on knees and elbows, in an athlete's posture so ancient, so mythic that I have no words for it.

Amby's mum is still in Canberra so I am to replace her on Sunday for the preliminary final as the oranges and snakes provider. During the week I proudly mention this to my Newcastle friend. He laughs: 'The Oranges and Snakes Lady? Sounds like a figure from a Tarot card.' I approach my duty with religious solemnity—what sort of oranges? And how many? Is one per boy enough? Should I slice them in quarters or sixths? And the snakes for three-quarter time—will I get Natural brand with less sugar? But isn't their whole purpose to administer a sugar rush that will blast the boys through to the final siren?

My anxiety levels on the day are such that when Amby and his dad are ready to go I still haven't finished cutting the fruit. They leave without me. On his way out the door Amby hugs me hard and mutters, 'I'm gonna kill 'em. I'm gonna *kill* 'em.' Is this the moment when he passes his fear to me, to hold?

Using my Melways I blunder out to West Essendon, park my car in the mountainous grounds of St Bernard's College, and lug my heavy basket to the verge of the oval. It lies at the base of an excavated area. Unless I'm hallucinating with nerves, half a hillside has been carved away to make room for footy.

It's a bright spring day, high clouds, gentle air. Everyone's revved up, in manic mood. Silas's dad and I go in search of the boys. The team we're versing, Hoppers Crossing, is making a hell of a racket in the pavilion corridor. We pass them with lowered eyes and enter the room where the Colts are waiting.

For a second I think I'm going to keel over.

They are huge.

Even the shorter, slighter, younger ones tower over me—Ned! Harvey! Joey! When did you get so big? They are crammed into the bare concrete room, milling about, a thicket of shoulders and torsos and thighs—striped tops and white shorts, boots of every colour, mullets and cropped heads and tousled crowns of hair, enormous faces and eyes and teeth, and thundering voices. I stand on the threshold with my basket, like Little Red Riding Hood at the edge of the forest.

The air in the room is bright with tension: they are raring to go.

I can't see Boof but he must be in here somewhere, buried among the taller ones, firing them up. They lurch apart and I catch a glimpse of his dense black curls, his resolute face. Archie speaks to them low and urgent: 'Every single one of us is gonna *run all day*.' I can't hear what Remy says; something is deafening me—excitement and fear. They hold a pause for Angus in the corner to make a shy little speech about going for goal, then they throw their arms round each other in a ring to roar their chorus, and rush out past me like a dam breaking. I flatten myself against the wall, and down the concrete staircase to the ground they pour, their studded boots clattering sharp as horses' hooves.

Fitzy kicks the first goal. They rush to him, smother

him in praise. From the moment I see his face, flustered, incredulous among the buffeting bodies, the match becomes a blur. The notebook and pencil die in my hands. I remember it only in disconnected flashes. Meth's mum, turning to me open-mouthed at her son's smooth curving run. Harvey kicking three goals in a row: bang, bang, bang. Fierce fast tackling, bodies sprawling or somersaulting and springing back to their feet. Girls near me shouting, 'Am-bee! Am-bee!'

A woman screaming; it might be me.

Boof's mum: 'Watch out, Helen—you'll have a heart attack!'

Mad laughter. 'I can think of worse ways to die.'

At half-time my sister and I take out the oranges, offering the plastic box, whispering, 'Glory—glory to you.' The giant boys shaking their heads or seizing and gulping at handfuls of fruit.

Third quarter. We're ahead, we're further ahead. Jake wins a tackle, kicks another goal from the free; his dad on the sidelines sees him put on a provocative little strut and shouts a warning, 'No! No!' but three Hoppers Crossing boys lose their tempers and one of them runs into Jake full tilt. Angus flares up to back him and it's on. Whistles shrilling. They're sending Angus off!

And a slowed-down scene, like a street photo outside a night club: long-legged Angus, upright, pale, arms spread wide, leaning back against a wall of boys who are hustling him off the field. Boof, with the calm skill of a bouncer, has cut him out of the brawl and turned him around towards the coach's box: Boof the peacemaker, bent far forward, almost crouching beside his taller teammate, his bright face peeping up at the level of Angus's armpit, as if about to heave him off the ground.

Angus ambles into the little shelter shed, trying for nonchalance, and sits on the bench. His penalty is only fifteen minutes, a yellow card not a red one: he'll be able to play next Sunday if we make it through today.

And, my God, I think we're going to. A beat before the end of the third quarter, Joey marks the ball on the boundary in the left forward pocket. The siren blares. The game stops. Everyone freezes to watch this skinny kid line up his set shot. From the Hoppers Crossing supporters rises a thin, mocking wail. We hear Joey's boot meet the leather and the ball soars thirty metres beautifully, perfectly, right between the big sticks. His teammates rush howling to him and sweep him off his feet.

Colts blaze into the final quarter with fearless strength and grit, astonishing their parents, who can't hold in their glee. We win, 77:42. People stagger about laughing, wiping their eyes, marvelling to each other. We've never done it before! We're *in the grand final.*

I have a dozen juicy pieces of orange left in my container. I offer them randomly to every passer-by. Many accept; but I make the mistake of holding out the box to a mother and son who, I realise too late, must be with the other team. The mother makes a confused murmuring sound, not meeting my eye, and the boy hits me with a cold death stare.

A man with a drooping grey moustache walks past and shouts over his shoulder at Boof's mum, 'Yeah, all right, you had a better team than us, but that umpire was biased—that fat guy!'

'He was not!' she retorts, struggling along with her arms full of equipment and great bunches of blue and yellow streamers. 'He did a really good job! And I haven't noticed *you* volunteering.'

He slouches off, snarling.

She looks at me with a shrug. 'We get a lot of that. You get used to it.'

We go home in two cars. Amby's dad, with Amby all euphoric and oblivious beside him, pulls out of the carpark past me. He rolls down the window and mutters to me in a low, disgusted voice, 'Did you hear?'

'What?'

'The Bulldogs *lost*. To *West Coast*.'

He drops into gear and surges away up the hill. He's devastated. How come I'm not? Can these boys be usurping the place in my heart that's been held for twenty years by the mighty Western Bulldogs?

As people wander away blissfully from St Bernard's, the word goes around that the club has reserved a couple of tables upstairs at Hardiman's pub in Kensington. Food will be available and everyone is invited to go back for a drink, to celebrate.

Amby's dad has gone home to lick his wounds, but Amby and I agree to head for the party. When we walk in through the downstairs bar, the whole building is levitating with footy.

Big screens pump out an AFL game with the volume up high. We climb the stairs and pause on the threshold of the upper room.

The U16 boys are crammed together at three big tables way down the far end, gutsing pizza. The fathers and male team officials are standing in a big loose circle at the top end of the room, drinking beer and talking hard. All the women present—manager, mothers, nannas, teenage sisters—are hovering on their feet halfway between the two groups, with their backs to the men and their gazes resting adoringly on their boys gorging at the tables.

Jake's elegant mum is standing near me, holding a glass of wine; she looks at me with a wry expression. She nods towards the boys, then over her shoulder at the group of men. She raises her eyebrows: 'Classic, isn't it?' 'It's a time warp! It's the 1950s!' We crack up. Amby makes a dive for his teammates. Xavier's dad, the assistant coach, wanders into the room. He drifts to a central table at which Boof's mum and a couple of other mothers and I have managed to score some chairs. We smile up at him. He hesitates beside our spot, vaguely greets us, then, drawn by a centripetal masculine force, ducks away towards the players' tables.

—

At nightfall I go into the kitchen next door and settle on the couch with Smokey the dog while Amby's dad, as always, makes the dinner. I'm so tired after the strained, victorious day that I'm not capable of conversation. And I find that conversation is not required. Amby's dad has been keeping a grip on his rage and disillusionment about the Bulldogs' shaming loss for hours, so as not to cast shade on his son's jubilation. But now that Amby is in his bedroom with the door shut, shouting and laughing on his phone, his father is free to let fly; and he does, in a stream of pained, coherent, deeply informed analysis and criticism that builds to a declaration: the coach, the one who since 2015 has taken the Bulldogs to two grand finals and one premiership, must resign.

I lie on the couch at the dim end of the room, between the bookcase and the silent TV, and let his tirade of anger and sorrow flow past me. I see that he is heartbroken. There's nothing I can say. Nothing is required of me but company. How deep it goes in men, this bond, this loyalty: I would never mock it. I remember a man once saying to me, 'I can't afford to follow a team. I mean I can't *psychically* afford it. To deal with their failures and losses.' I doze and wake and doze again. The sleeping dog's warm back rests against my hip; I stroke the stringy tendons of his hind legs and the coarse, dry pads of his paws, and Amby's dad at the kitchen bench laments and grieves. And yet all the while he goes on performing without resentment his daily service: chopping vegetables with the cleaver, deftly dismembering the chicken, sliding the heavy pans across the stovetop: working, with a father's patient devotion, to feed his family.

—

On the Monday after the preliminary final win, Amby comes home from school and says he doesn't think he'll go to training tonight: 'I'm sore all over, from yesterday.'

His dad and I exchange a look. Which of us will say it? We speak over each other: 'You have to go, Amb. Aren't you a captain? Before the grand final? You can't not go. It's a no-brainer. You have to be with your team.'

He picks up his bag.

The only people out on the oval when we get there are two old blokes having a quiet kick. Amby slopes off and I stop near the recycle bins to watch them. They must be in their seventies, blocky and shapeless, a bald one in a red T-shirt and shorts, a white-haired one in a black tracksuit. The light is fading and they plod back and forth in the dimness, stooped, stiff-legged, silent, kicking low and slow, trying to mark, often missing. They can hardly raise their arms, and they don't want to run; when they have to, their movements are awkward and narrow, constrained I suppose by joint pain. They are so absorbed in their play that they don't notice I'm there. My heart is 'strangely warmed'. I feel for them. I envy them. I long to duck under the rail and ask them to let me join in. No way in the world would I do such a thing.

And I remember with a melancholy regret the secret resolution I made on the very first night I came to pre-season training: that I would not pick up and return the balls that flew over the boundary and into the skate park. At the time I came up with a self-righteous feminist rationale: I would not be their mother, their grandmother, or their servant. Nor would I suck up to them or try to be their friend. I would stand back, detach and observe. I would be a witness, and that was all. The true reason, of course, is that I had not kicked a footy in seventy years. I have forgotten how, and I'm afraid that if I try I will make a fool of myself and people will laugh at me.

I take up my possie on the high back of my bench. It's dark now, the tall lights flick on. The women jog past, a dozen of them, in their lycra and their bright headlamps.

On the oval the boys are high from yesterday's win, laughing, razzing. Angus tries to yank Remy's shorts down. A boy casts himself on his back on the grass and lies there, knees bent. 'Why,' says Archie, 'are you stargazing? At footy training?' They forge into handball drill, bellowing each other's names.

A man and woman, regulars, pause in their walk to watch the boys at work. The man asks eagerly, 'Are these boys in the final this week?'

'Yes,' I say, 'the *grand* final.'

'Who are they playing?'

'Newport.'

'I'll have to look 'em up!' he says. 'Good luck!'

—

All week I keep noticing that I'm not hungry. Am I coming down with something? My heart's beating too fast. There's a big empty hole under my ribs. I can't get enough air to fill it. It takes me till Thursday training, the last one for the season, to twig what the matter is. 'You've got *sport nerves*,' says Archie's mum, at the boundary rail. Our laughter is rather shrill.

Harvey's mum shows me a photo of his knee, taken right after he got hit in the last match sim—a horrible big fat swelling. I gasp and clap my hands over my mouth. She is unruffled: 'His dad and I are both pharmacists. It's gone way down. We've got the crystals on to it.'

I hear distant splinters of what Archie is telling the boys before they part till Sunday.

'Don't kick high. Just bomb it along the ground for all I care.

'Get it forward. Kick to grass. Kick to space—use space. Just get it forward, so Fitzy can get a hold of it.

'They're big blokes, but they're slow.

'We're gonna run and run and *run*.

'There's gonna be about a thousand people watching you—you've got to be LOUD.

'And don't go out on Saturday night. *Don't go out!*'

In the kitchen Amby and I pore over the team photo, talking about injuries.

'Did you see Harvey's knee?' I say. 'It was awful. All bulging. Is he strong?'

'Harvey? Harvey's *really* strong. I used to test myself against different kids at training—you know, bump them hard, see what happens. Mostly I could push them out of my way, but when I did it to Harvey he was so solid I bounced off about four metres. And he just stood still.'

But oh God—they've got to face Newport again. Those

weighty, glowering guys. A fortnight ago on their home ground they rolled over us like a tank. Thrashed us by forty points. They'll be ready to do it again. I bet they've regrouped and massively focused and spent two weeks in the gym. What if the Colts are too light-bodied and slight to stand up to them? Oh, they're going to kill us. It's going to be a massacre.

I try to distract myself with old copies of the *New Yorker*, but everything I read forces me back to the game. In a review of a novel about soldiers: 'the body under stress is heroic, living in its wholeness, with consciousness remaining intact, even when vibrating in pain'. Someone asks James Baldwin about talent: 'I know a lot of talented ruins. Beyond talent lie all the usual words: discipline, love, luck, but, most of all, endurance.'

What will our boys have to endure on Sunday?

—

On Saturday Amby and his brother and I go to the cafe for breakfast. Amby is wondering whether to have his hair cut before or after tomorrow's game. I control an urge to say, 'Do NOT cut your hair! Haven't you heard of Samson?'

'If I do it on Monday it'll be looking good by Wednesday and Thursday.'

'What's on Wednesday or Thursday? A date?'

He laughs, and frowns. The boys get out their phones and compare possible hairstyles. Amby shows me the one he likes.

'It's good,' I say. 'It's like what you've got now, but shorter at the back and slightly thinned out.'

His brother, who is sporting a two-week-old buzz cut, examines it with a wry twist of the lips: 'Nah.'

'Why?'

'It's not…edgy.'

'I don't want to be edgy,' says Amby. 'I don't want to look tough.'

'Don't you want to look scary?' says his brother.

'What would scary mean?' I say. 'Like you'd commit violence if you had to?'

Neither of them comes up with an answer.

'Show her the Edgar,' says his brother.

Amby holds out his phone. I give a cry of revulsion. 'The Edgar,' says the website, 'comes with a mid to high skin fade with short thick hair on top and a little length in the front. The *fringe* is combed forward and down to cover part of the forehead. The hairstyle is fashionable, ruggedly handsome and bold. It will make you look clean-cut with an attitude.'

'You're not *contemplating* that, are you?'

'Course not.'

'Are you thinking a lot about tomorrow's game?'

'Yep.'

'Would it be better to concentrate on something else? Until the time comes?'

'No. I need to think about the other ruckman. I have to think of…'

'Tactics?'

'How to neutralise him. I have to *neutralise* him.'

'How? Timing?'

'Yes, timing. Jump earlier so I can get on top of him.'

'Like what your dad says? "Ka-boom"? The other guy jumps on *boom* but you jump on *ka*?'

'Yeah. Plus I have to make sure I get 50/50 ruck tap.'

What the hell is 50/50 ruck tap? This is not the moment to ask.

Oh, I hope tomorrow won't be one of those desperate crawling games where the players writhe in piles on the ground. I long for what they call 'a good clean running game of footy'. I want to shout to them: 'Get up and run! So I can admire you!'

—

My daughter has polished off her work in Canberra and rushed home. Early in the morning she and Amby sit close together on the couch. It's hard to see who is holding and who is being held. They are borderless, boundaryless, for comfort and to welcome home a mother who has been away for six weeks, during which time I have done my best to fill her space.

—

The game is at St Bernard's—the dramatically excavated private-school sportsground on which we beat Hoppers Crossing last Sunday in the preliminary final. It's a cool spring day. People are arriving hours early. Everything I look at seems to be hovering a few inches above 'the floor'.

Not knowing where to put ourselves, Amby's mum and

I go for a walk around the ground. On the grass behind the southern goal I spot a dead rat, delicately eviscerated by some other creature, its entrails spread on the grass in a sinister shape. I am drawn to it with superstitious dread, but she won't even look at it.

Meth's mum in her pretty white puffer jacket arrives with the oranges and snakes. A man cuddling his tiny daughter on a picnic rug tries to explain the game to her: 'See, they have to *get* that ball, and then—' The U16s' parents and siblings and aunts and uncles and grandparents and schoolmates and girlfriends are faithfully rolling up, forming into nervy circles near the boundary, craning their necks towards the pavilion in which the two teams are secluded in their separate chambers, preparing themselves for battle.

The building is teeming with boys and men running importantly up and down and in and out. There's a tense, low hum. I fight my way up the stairs. The door to the visitors' room is shut but I can hear the Colts' muffled cries. Archie is conferring in the hallway with Silas, their heads together, their backs to me, the boy pleading, the coach intent. I shouldn't be here. I brake behind them, just close enough to hear Silas say, earnestly: 'I'm on today, Arch—I promise. Keep me forward?'

I bolt towards the stairs. A Colts father goes steaming past me. 'Boof's up there!' he shouts. 'Boof's back!'

Down on the grass Boof's dad, who can't stop laughing, spots my notebook and says, 'Don't forget to put in the dads who fly their sons home from Darwin!'

Fitzy's dad, the GP and trainer, walks briskly past us,

carrying in one hand a light metal frame with cloth straps: oh Lord, is that a stretcher?

Up near the grandstand Harvey's mum is handing out bunches of streamers for us to wave when the team runs out: some of the mothers have made a paper banner on bamboo poles for them to burst through.

And here they come, our boys, pounding down the steps and through the narrow gate, they don't see us or know us and we don't expect them to, and I'm so busy flourishing my streamers and shouting 'Go Colts!', while Newport in their ominous black spread out into their positions, that I miss the rending of the banner, and see only the Colts' retreating backs and the shreds of blue paper fluttering to the grass on the wind of their passing.

The officials in yellow march on to the ground, an umpire holding the ball aloft in one hand on a rigidly vertical arm: the hieratic gesture that for a breathless moment hushes the crowd.

The siren, the bounce, the ruckmen leap, and my brain—till now sharply focused and registering—stutters, misfires, and conks out. The usually thin crowd of Colts supporters is now a dense mob, and it's yelling for its boys. I can't hear anything, I can't think, I can't *see*! Where's Amby's dad? I have to get near him or I'm lost. I push along the line till I find him.

'What's happening? What's happening?'

'This ground,' he shouts, 'is bigger than the one they beat us on! Last time they swamped us, remember? They completely crowded us, we had no room to move—our fast ones were stopped before they could get going—but this ground's wider. Look! We can run!'

First quarter the teams go neck and neck. Quarter time and Newport are one point in front, 20:19. Half-time and we're two points ahead, 41:39. I run out to the huddle, where my mind still works: the boys' hands plunging into the box of snakes and oranges, their eyes fixed and staring, Amby's nose sprouting a plug of blood-soaked cottonwool, Archie's face white-cheeked and tense among the clustered heads. The siren blasts. The team stands tight around their coach. 'Back our running power, boys,' he shouts. 'We can win this if we have the willingness to match their big bodies.'

'This is it,' mutters a man at the rail. 'It'll be the third quarter that decides it.'

And the Colts are willing. Those big Newport bodies are starting to flag: they're tiring, they're slowing down, and as they falter, the Colts show what they're made of. Is this what footy is for? The pure thing, the point of it? They're a team now, in the full sense of the word: they know each other, they trust each other, they've made a tough and flexible fabric, and the fabric is holding.

'Will you look at Boof?' shouts Amby's dad, elated. 'He bloody owns that back line! He can really read the play. He watches the ball come in, he predicts where it'll land, he's ready for it and he turns it into an attack! And Silas in the forward line—he's the lighthouse! He's what we needed! He's kicking goal after goal! And they're all from marks—big strong contested marks!'

Three-quarter time, we're twenty-two points ahead, 62:40. The Colts pace about, squinting in the bright sun: they're as high as kites. The warning siren, and they press close around Archie. 'We've got twenty more minutes of our season, boys, and it comes down to this: every single one of you has to match their physicality. And when we run, we *run*! We run in waves!'

They hush for Boof: 'Let's leave *nothing in the tank*. Let's let 'em hear it.' His colossal voice from deep in the huddle: '*COLTS—ON—THREE*.' The boys' staccato reply: '*One two three COLTS!*'

Newport are game. They fight on. We haven't scored yet in the final quarter. They kick two goals and two behinds, but still they're trailing. Amby shoulders out of a thick contest, kicks high but too wide: *nooooo!* The ball soars across the boundary and plummets down towards the Colts crowd. Girls scatter and squeal, and Amby's brother, with an ironical smile, stands still and marks it neatly on his chest, like a frog swallowing a fly. Are we laughing or crying? Silas kicks our last goal, his fifth for the match. 68:54. They can't beat us now. Liam bursts off the bench calling for the ball but Amby is tearing down the wing with it, bouncing it, bouncing it. His kick, the game's last one, misses and veers across the face of goal, and it doesn't matter, because there's the final siren and the Colts have won.

Have won!

Are the *Premiers*.

Archie strides on to the ground, white as plaster. He keeps his back to the screaming supporters but I can see the tears on his cheeks. People weep, pretend not to be weeping, seize each other in violent hugs. We laugh maniacally, doubled over as if in pain.

The teams mingle on the field, high-five, shake hands; the captains and the coaches speak their gracious words. The whole milling crowd swarms to the river side of the ground. A big circle of spectators forms around the two lines of players. I'm squashed behind tall people, I worm my way through.

Speeches, but I'm too dazed and deaf to hear. The cheering. The presentation ritual: each boy is called forward alone to shake a smiling official's hand, bow his head, and have a medal hung round his neck on a pale-blue ribbon. But one player of the defeated team turns away from the official, reaches up to the nape of his neck and draws the ribbon over his head, crushes it in one hand, and walks back to his place in the line, with his hand hanging by his side, the medal and the ribbon invisible in his fist. Another does the same, and another, and another, almost all of them. 'They must have really believed they were going to win,' whispers a Colts dad beside me. 'They must have thought they *deserved* to win.' I'm shocked by my silent rush of empathy with their gesture, which I have never seen before—what is it? Is it 'unsportsmanlike', and angry, and bitter? Or is it dignified, a sign of humility, an acceptance of fate? Oh, it is so unbearably painful to be congratulated for not having won.

But the brightly polished two-handled silver cup, raised by Remy and Jake, surges up into the late afternoon sun, and blazes in it.

As if a spell has been broken, the Newport side and its

supporters melt away. They dematerialise, they are gone. The Colts crowd, too, is dispersing, but more reluctantly: nobody wants to leave the place where it happened.

Our boys, these warriors, emerge from the rooms with their bags of gear. Their families long to envelop them; but even in their street clothes, returned to normal size, they are transformed: radiating such charisma, such flushed, wordless, incredulous ecstasy, that we ordinary mortals hardly dare to touch them.

Small children are out on the ground now, screaming and tumbling and racing about. Everybody wants to hug Archie. His older brother and two young sisters, while they wait for him, are having a quiet kick together on the oval; he's dying to get out there and join them. 'Include me!' he shouts. '*Include me!*'

Angus is standing on his own, just inside the boundary. I risk it: 'Angus. Well played, dear. Congratulations.'

He stirs from his reverie, looks down at me from his six foot two, and gently takes my hand. 'You were there, weren't you,' he says, 'right from the start. I've been meaning to come and talk to you. I want you to tell Ambrose from me to keep going with his footy. He played a great game today. He'll do well.'

When almost everyone else has drifted away, a boy with a cap of thick dark curls sits by himself on the bottom step of the grandstand, leaning forward, elbows pressed into his thighs, looking out over the close-mown turf. Amby's mum and I approach him reverently.

'Boof. Thank God you came back. We salute you.'

He looks up, too drained to speak, and slowly, formally, offers his hand.

In a week or so, with all due ceremony, at our suburb's lawn bowls club, there will be awards and prize-givings and signings of jumpers with Sharpies, an announcement of the over-subscribing of the Bring Boof Home GoFundMe, of Boof's family's donation of the overflow so the boys can keep their jumpers in memory of their achievement instead of giving them back to the club. Archie will make a witty, affectionate speech that describes and honours each boy in turn. But tonight there will be riotous celebrations, beers in somebody's backyard, outrageous texts and phone calls, singing and yelling and laughing and apologising to passers-by on the suburb's streets and in its pizza and kebab shops. Remy will smoke a cigar.

And it's not until I'm halfway up the steep grassy bank between the oval and the parked cars, following Amby in his silent bliss, and plodding slowly behind the rest of my family like the old woman that I am, pausing to get my breath, hauling myself along by grabbing a low branch whenever I reach a tree, that my dream comes shimmering back to me, the one I had the night before the preliminary final, the dream which, in my superstition, I censored, never told to a single soul, and forced myself to forget: the Colts in triumphal parade, captains at their head, marching in wedge formation down the Champs-Elysées at dusk, all of them tall, robust and magnificent, chins high, shoulders back, arms swinging free—and behind them a sky on fire with brilliantly curlicued, cartwheeling starbursts of light.